GW00361067

If Trees Could Talk

The story of woodlands around Belfast

C. Barrel 03

Veteran oak by the motte, Belvoir Park.

If Trees Could Talk

The story of woodlands around Belfast

Ben Simon

2009

THE FOREST OF
BELFAST

ISBN 978-0-9551583-2-2

A publication of the Forest of Belfast
4-10 Linenhall Street, Belfast BT2 8BP

Text © the author
Photographs © as indicated in the picture credits

Design by Cheah Design
Printed by W&G Baird

Published with the support of:

Contents

Acknowledgements

This publication was researched and written as a contribution to the work of the Forest of Belfast Initiative, the urban forestry partnership for the Greater Belfast area. The Forest of Belfast includes government, local authorities, voluntary environmental organisations and individuals and I am very grateful for the support and encouragement given to this exploration of Belfast's trees by all of the members of the Steering Group.

I would like to thank Sue Christie of Northern Ireland Environment Link for her insightful comments in discussions about the structure and content of this book and Martin Walsh, Helen McCallan and Robert Scott for commenting on a draft of the book. Many people contributed to my knowledge of city trees: in particular I would like to mention Fiona Holdsworth, Alan McHaffie and Reg Maxwell of Belfast City Council Parks and Cemeteries Services, Brian McNeill of Estate and Forestry Services, landscape architects Robert Carson and Brian Woods, environmental consultants Roy Anderson and Dermot Hughes. Staff of many environmental organisations kindly provided information including Ian Humphreys of Conservation Volunteers NI, Tim Duffy of Colin Glen Trust and Peter Cush of Northern Ireland Environment Agency. Forest Service kindly provided access to their extensive records of tree planting. I am grateful to Terence Reeves-Smyth of the Built Heritage Directorate of Northern Ireland Environment Agency and to Mike Baillie and David Brown of Queen's University School of Geography, Archaeology and Palaeoecology for their interest and helpful comments about my research and to David Brown for dating timber samples collected from fallen trees in Belfast.

Staff at archives and libraries were extremely helpful and put up with my constant requests over a three-year period to view material. In particular I would like to mention the help given in Belfast by the staff of the newspaper archive and local history sections of the Central Library, the Linenhall Library, the Public Record Office of Northern Ireland (PRONI) and Queen's University Library. Maura Pringle, cartographer at Queen's University School of Geography, Archaeology and Palaeoecology, and Michelle Ashmore and Paul Hackney of the Ulster Museum were also of great assistance. My research at Dublin was aided by staff at the National Library, Royal Irish Academy and Trinity College libraries. In London, staff at the National Archive at Kew and British Library (Rare Books and Maps) were also very willing to respond to my many enquiries.

The financial support provided by Better Belfast, Northern Ireland Environment Agency, Belfast City Council, Ulster Garden Villages and Crann, Ireland's tree charity, is gratefully acknowledged.

I also thank all my friends who put up with me endlessly talking about the trees of Belfast. Special thanks to Alexandra De La Torre for her encouragement and support.

Ben Simon, September 2009

1. Discovering our woodland heritage

Walking around the centre of Belfast today it is difficult to envisage the landscape of 400 years ago when the Lagan Valley was largely woodland and Arthur Chichester, who had been granted a huge landholding in the region, was starting to develop a planned town. A report about this project written around 1611 described land being 'plotted out' and the construction of timber houses with chimneys, an inn said to have very good lodgings and a castle of local brick built on the remains of an earlier fortification.

Redevelopment over the centuries has removed all traces of the buildings in Chichester's town, including his castle, which is only recalled by the names of streets close to where it stood: Castle Place and Castle Lane. There is also nothing left to help us picture the former extensive gardens of the castle, which were centred on the area where today the clothes shops, chemists, bookshops and burger bars of Donegall Place do business.

In the second half of the 18th century Belfast was still a small town. There was a garden of cherry trees where the City Hall now stands, and Lower Ormeau, the district around the Gasworks, was Cromac Wood, a place of oak trees and the haunt of swans. One link we do still have to this lost landscape is the route of one of the original passes that cut through Cromac Wood, the road known as Donegall Pass.

In the heart of the city the oldest patches of greenery to be found today are the formal grounds around a few civic buildings such as the trees and grass at Clifton House in Clifton Street, built as the Poorhouse and opened in 1774; and at Belfast Academical Institution (Inst), which was founded in 1810. Our best known city space, the lawns behind the screen of lime and sycamore trees at the City Hall, is only just over 100 years old.

Since the 1970s new tree-lined public squares have been planned and developed in the central area. First were Cathedral Gardens by the Art College and Jubilee Garden at Victoria Street. Then Writers' Square at Saint Anne's Cathedral, open space by the Albert Clock and Custom House in Laganside, and at other focal points including Blackstaff Square (Amelia Street) and Bankmore Square (Dublin Road).

Walking from the city centre, your path is often under street trees that have been planted since the 1980s. This planting project has transformed the appearance of many of the shopping streets and arterial routes around Belfast. Take a glance at the shapes and colours of these trees and you will soon notice that a surprisingly wide range of tree species now enhance the city. Starting from the City Hall, if you go down Linenhall Street you walk under Turkish hazel with neat, conical crowns interspersed with some cherry trees that have a more open network of branches. Along adjacent Bedford Street at one end are white-barked birch trees and at the other hornbeam with dark coloured trunks and a pyramidal cluster of ascending branches. At the junction with Ormeau Avenue, the red sandstone fountain on the traffic island is surrounded by four whitebeam trees, a species distinguished by the silver-white underside of the leaves.

Reaching Dublin Road you can see evidence of street trees planted over generations including some old, tall, London plane trees, younger lime trees and, in Shaftesbury Square, young maple and birch trees.

A short way further into the south of the city, you can get away from the hustle and bustle and relax in some of Belfast's oldest parks and public spaces, including Ormeau Park (formerly the grounds of the early 19th century residence of the Donegall family) and the Botanic Garden (founded in 1828 on land that had previously been a plant nursery). The Botanic Garden connects with other open space at Methodist College (Methody), the grounds surrounding the Queen's University Lanyon building, and the Theological College at the end of Botanic Avenue - institutions built during the 19th century in fields outside Belfast.

You can find greenery in unexpected places in the inner city, such as the trees that lean over the high walls of Clifton Street Graveyard on the lower Antrim Road and Friar's Bush Graveyard in Stranmillis. These city spaces are valued by residents and have interesting plant life, including occasional large elms that so far have managed to survive the destruction wrought by Dutch elm disease. Friar's Bush is also the home of an elderly thorn tree which, by reputation, is the tree that gave rise to the name of the graveyard, under which a friar is said to have prayed and been killed. However, in many heavily built up suburban areas there is little public open space, a problem made worse by a lack of gardens in streets of back-to-back terraces. This is particularly noticeable in Ballymacarrett and around the lower Falls, Shankill and Crumlin Roads.

We are fortunate in Belfast to have the Lagan Valley Regional Park with its riverside towpath and Colin Glen, places where one can walk by water through woods and meadows until the city is left far behind. Another linear walkway that connects the city with its suburbs has been developed along the old Comber railway line in east Belfast. Creating new greenways takes years of hard work and discussion with landowners, communities and planners. However, work will soon be under way to link up open space to complete long-distance routes along the Three Mile Water in Newtownabbey and by the Connswater to connect Victoria Park with the steep public path up Cregagh Glen in the Castlereagh Hills. These river valleys are great places to discover built heritage including the magnificent, huge railway bridges over the Three Mile Water and, at the other extreme, the delightful little arched bridge over the Connswater near Elmgrove Primary School, which is one of Belfast's forgotten treasures, a real link to our past as it is most likely one of the city's oldest surviving stone structures.

Further from the city centre there are more public spaces in Victorian suburbs such as Falls Park, Alexandra Park and at the Waterworks. There is also extensive open space at the City Cemetery on Falls Road, which is now being cleared of dense vegetation to reveal a fascinating heritage of gravestone inscriptions. The more prosperous Victorian suburbs are notable for their large houses surrounded by spacious gardens, areas which often gain the title (or rather Belfast put-down) of being leafy suburbs. These are most obvious in Malone, though large gardens with beautiful mature trees are also a feature of other areas such as Bloomfield, Belmont, parts of Holywood, Cultra, Jordanstown and a few remaining parts of the Shore Road in Newtownabbey that have escaped redevelopment. These are places that still exhibit the Victorian love of exotic conifers with trees like giant redwood (Wellingtonia), monkey puzzle, Monterey cypress, cedars and pines towering over the old redbrick villas.

Most gardens in the suburbs are surrounded by evergreen hedges that add welcome year round colour. In the older gardens there are often fully grown colourful exotic shrubs like rhododendron and magnolia, the latter particularly noticeable in gardens along University Square when they are in full flower in April. Probably the oldest garden trees are two sweet chestnut at Cranmore, hidden away but growing well in woodland that can be glimpsed from the Malone Road; these are thought to have been planted before 1700. It is possible that there are a few other trees of this age around Belfast in long-established gardens, still flourishing though their history is forgotten by all.

Beautiful avenues of majestic street trees can be discovered in some suburbs. The majority are limes, including the impressive rows to be found on Eglantine Avenue and Malone Park in south Belfast. Sometimes more unusual street trees were planted, such as the Austrian pines on the pavements of Cyprus

Avenue in east Belfast. Most of our pavement plantings are of one or two species, though sometimes someone with a different approach had a hand, such as at Hampton Park near the top of the Ormeau Road where one can find a mix of mature horse chestnut, lime, sweet chestnut, beech and maple street trees. If you want to see how impressive avenue planting can be, take a trip to the magnificent double row of lime trees at Stormont, a planting project started in 1929 and completed in 1932. A much shorter but still notable avenue of trees is formed by the twelve giant redwood with massive trunks and tapering stems which can be seen from the Upper Lisburn Road lining the private driveway into Hunterhouse College.

Some old demesnes still survive in the outer suburbs around Belfast. These were originally developed as private landscaped grounds around a big house, and today are some of best places to find mature woodland with typical woodland plants and wildlife such as badgers. Two good examples are the woodlands at Cave Hill Country Park and at Rathfern on the eastern slopes of Carnmoney Hill, both places where there was extensive planting in the 19th century and which today have networks of public footpaths to walk and, through gaps in the trees, discover great views over Belfast. Any tour of Belfast's woods must include the Stormont Estate in east Belfast, where there are formal landscaped grounds, woodland blocks and remnants of more natural woodland in valleys behind the Parliament Building. In the Lagan Valley south of Belfast a number of demesnes have survived largely intact, including two that are public parks (Malone, now Barnett Demesne and Wilmont, now Sir Thomas and Lady Dixon Park). Much of the former walled grounds of Belvoir Park have also been preserved as Belvoir Park Golf Club and the adjacent Belvoir Park Forest.

In north Down, two areas of woodland at Redburn and Crawfordsburn have been developed as Country Parks managed by the Northern Ireland Environment Agency. Also in north Down you can explore the most impressive of our estate landscapes, the legacy left by the first Marquis of Dufferin and Ava in the area between Helen's Bay, Craigantlet and Clandeboye. Much of the estate is private but the plantations, shelter belts, rides and hill tops crowned with circular woods that he planted can be seen from the attractive tree-lined path that was once the Marquis's route through his estate to the coast. This is now a public walkway that can be accessed from a number of places, including via a door at the bottom of the subway steps of Helen's Bay railway station. Walking through this dark concrete underpass to enter into a wonderful woodland must rank as one of our most bizarre and unusual gateways to the natural world.

For those who want to go for a walk amongst the giants, the best places to discover old trees are in the old demesnes, most notably at Belvoir Park. Here there are veteran oaks, several with a circumference of over 5m; the largest, Granddad, is a massive, squat, hollow tree with a circumference of 8.8m at just above ground level, making it one of the largest oaks in Ireland.

Belfast's woodlands are a living classroom where one can discover not only ancient trees and diverse wildlife, but also gain insights into the ways that people have, generation after generation, managed these landscapes. For example, at Cave Hill the remnants of the walls of a deer park, constructed over 300 years ago, can still be traced. Sometimes in woods and demesnes one comes across lines of stately old trees which were most likely planted along the boundaries of fields that have long since disappeared. Areas of parkland developed as grazed grassland with widely spaced tall trees can also be identified in many former demesnes, though these landscapes are often obscured by more recent plantings. Studying the diversity of woodland life, including the trees, plants, invertebrates and fungi, provides additional evidence towards our understanding of the fascinating and complex history of these places.

Heading still further out of Belfast into farmland, have a look at the field hedgerows. They are a place to search out occasional veteran trees but also check if they are dominated by hawthorn or something less expected like beech. In parts of the Antrim Hills to the north and west of Belfast and to the north of Newtownabbey long-established field hedges of beech (sometimes with spaced Scots pine) are surprisingly common. Beech hedges are an attractive sight in autumn and winter, when their leaves turn golden-brown, though it is a puzzle why beech was the hedge plant of choice for some farmers as it does not form a particularly stock-proof barrier.

Around old farmsteads groups of mature trees can often be seen, planted as shelter belts and to provide a ready supply of firewood. In the countryside trees are also common along little river valleys or steep slopes, places that were difficult to plough. Lone fairy thorns still stand in some farmers' fields, untouched because 'you never know what might happen.'

Yew trees were traditionally planted at graveyards and in country churchyards one can sometimes find magnificent old yews. The most noteworthy examples around Belfast are at Carnmoney churchyard, Drumbeg churchyard with its unusual arches of trained Irish yew (look for the stone commemorating the planting of the older four arches) and, strangest of all, the two tall twisted yews that stand guard at the door of Holy Trinity Church Drumbo. The grounds of the First Presbyterian Church in Dunmurry, located by the railway level crossing, are also worth a visit to look at the trees (including two tall false acacia in the beautiful woodland garden of the glebe) and to visit the old church with its wonderful 19th century stained glass window in memory of the McCance family, that depicts the trees, plants and a waterfall at Colin Glen.

Although people have modified much of the landscape around Belfast, some remnants of long established woodlands have, remarkably, survived. One such site is Belvoir Park, which has veteran trees that are most likely the last vestiges of an ancient lowland wood. A very different kind of long-established woodland occurs on steep slopes and gullies around Belfast including the area by the zoo known as Hazelwood, parts of Carnmoney Hill and Knockagh and some of the upland stream valleys in the Belfast and Castlereagh Hills. These are woods of hazel with some tall ash or oak which are at their best in spring, when the ground has a carpet of bluebells and other wildflowers. The patches of wet woodland with willow and alder that flourish along most stream banks in the lowlands make up another semi-natural habitat that adds to the landscape of places like the Bog Meadows and Lagan Meadows.

It is incredible how quickly self-seeded trees and plants can colonise land. Looking around Belfast you can see many trees that have grown not by the hand of man but by nature. For example, where uplands are no longer grazed such as on the eastern slopes of Carnmoney Hill, the fields are invaded by hawthorn, hazel, blackthorn and ash. Along the higher slopes of the Belfast Hills scattered stunted trees, mainly hawthorn with some willow and rowan, find a foothold. Near the coast gorse, broom and sea buckthorn, the latter conspicuous because of its clumps of orange berries, are spreading amongst the taller trees planted along the embankments of the motorway to Newtownabbey. The grass strips by the more inland motorways are being naturally populated by ash and oak along with hawthorn, whin and willow. In Belfast gardens self-seeded elder, sycamore and ash seedlings regularly appear to the annoyance of gardeners.

Some non-native species can become a problem in our woods, spreading and dominating local flora unless checked. This is particularly the case with laurel and rhododendron which were widely planted in Victorian times to provide colour and also cover for game birds. Dense thickets of these evergreen shrubs have become so common that woods where they are rare, such as at Barnett Demesne, can appear

Monkey Puzzle, Ormeau Road.

Carol Baird 94/100

strangely bare in winter. In many woods efforts are being made to control laurel and rhododendron by felling and treating the stumps to prevent regeneration. At Cave Hill Country Park attempts are also being made to prevent the spread of sycamore where it has been taking over biodiverse woodland. Another problem plant is Himalayan balsam which is rapidly spreading along river banks and encroaching into damp glades in woods.

The urban forest is also a follower of fashion, changing in appearance depending on which trees are promoted by garden gurus. The Victorian fascination for conifers has left us with a beautiful legacy of exotic trees in old gardens and estates. The cabbage palm *Cordyline australis* was probably first widely planted in the early 20th century and became a feature around Bangor and other coastal areas where winter frosts were rare, though the mild weather of recent years has allowed it to be grown throughout the region. Following the Second Word War the planting of ornamental cherry trees became popular, most noticeably at Merville Garden Village in Newtownabbey. Here the lines of cherry trees by the roads are a sight to gladden the heart when covered in pink blossom in spring. Castlewellan Gold (a hybrid cypress discovered at Castlewellan in County Down) became remarkably popular for hedging in the 1960s and 1970s but the need to regularly clip this fast growing forest tree has more recently made home owners wary of planting it. Another hybrid conifer called Robinson Gold that for a while was also popular as a hedging plant was discovered even closer to Belfast, at Belvoir Park in 1962. This tree was named after George Robinson, the forestry supervisor, who was clearing undergrowth when he noticed a small seedling with an unusual golden colour. He dug it out and took it home and when it grew it became the parent tree from which cuttings were taken. A recent addition to Belfast gardens that works well in our landscape is Himalayan birch (*Betula utilis* var. *Jacquemontii*) an attractive, compact tree with a very white stem and upward growing branches. This tree is set to become a classic, though another introduction, the variegated poplar (*Populus x candicans* 'Aurora') widely sold in local garden centres in the early 1980s because of the striking cream and pink tinged young foliage, is already a has-been as it loses its colour and shape unless it is regularly pruned and often suffers from canker.

The landscape over the lifetime of an oak

Recent research into the heritage of Belvoir Park that included tree ring studies to date fallen oaks has shown that the woods contain some extraordinary trees. Several of the oaks sampled started to grow in the 17th century, one dating from 1642; this is the oldest date so far found for any tree in a woodland in Ireland. It is a remarkable fact that during the period in which these trees have grown from little saplings to their present majestic form, Belfast has developed from the small settlement of timber houses by Chichester's castle to what it is now, a city surrounded by a growing metropolitan area.

The recognition of the importance of the woods at Belvoir Park provided the inspiration for this book, which looks at the vital role that trees, parks and open places have played, generation after generation, in the development of the landscape and character of Belfast. This is a complex history and includes times when there was extensive planting and times when there was widespread felling. Timber has however remained a valued material, and today there is also a growing appreciation of other ways that trees enhance the environment and our lives. Trees support biodiversity. We cherish woods as places for relaxation and play, somewhere 'to get away from it all'. Trees are used to screen unsightly views and to provide privacy and shelter around houses. By planting trees we can help reduce levels of greenhouse gases and there is growing interest in wood as a renewable energy source. Tree planting is recognised as offering a practical way for communities to improve their neighbourhoods.

The history of Belfast's trees can be unravelled from old maps, early newspaper advertisements, estate records, paintings and photographs. Interesting observations can also be found in the comments jotted down by visitors and in early county surveys and local history books. In the following chapters the trees in the landscape are examined century by century. Details are given about our veteran and landmark trees and our most important urban woods. Recent tree planting schemes, which will determine the landscapes to be viewed by future generations, are described. The story is told of how trees became what they are today, an essential and welcome part of our city, suburbs and countryside.

The largest girthed oak at Belvoir Park. Circumference 8.8m at a height of 0.1m.

Map of Ulster by Francis Jobson. This little-known map is of particular interest as the cartographer attempted to distinguish between woods with tall growing trees and areas of scrub.

Note that where ÿ Countries haue any timber growinge in ÿ they are marked with ÿ greater sorte of trees thus ℙ and where ÿ Countries are vnderwoded (viz) with beech, hasell, willowes and thorne, they are marked with a lesser sorte of trees thus ℙℙℙ

2. A look at the early landscape
1570-1700

The earliest period during which we can gain a clear impression of the landscape around Belfast is the late 16th century, when a number of sources include references to trees and woods. At this time, the main town in the region was Carrickfergus, the centre of English power. Belfast was to develop at the lowest crossing point on the River Lagan, a ford protected by a castle which was held by the O'Neills, who controlled much of south County Antrim and north County Down.

The best information we have about the landscape of northeastern Ireland at this time is from maps. These show woodland in the Lagan Valley, to the southeast of Lough Neagh and in mid County Down. In contrast, no significant woods are shown in northeast Down or southeast Antrim. Of particular interest are two little-known manuscript maps of Ulster by Francis Jobson which date from around the 1590s. Although his surveying has been criticised (Jobson later admitted that some areas were imperfectly examined as he was working 'every hour in danger to loose my head') in these maps he not only tried to show the distribution of woods, but differentiated between those areas with tall trees and those with underwood. It is not clear if the underwood was regularly cut (coppice) woodland or unmanaged scrub, though in one map Jobson provided a list of the underwood trees. He described them as comprising hazel, willows, thorn and also beech, a tall growing tree that he may have included in error.[1]

Jobson shows underwood trees as occupying the Lagan Valley and adjacent areas of northwest Down; underwood with some tall trees in mid-Down; and mainly tall trees in the area southeast of Lough Neagh, the land known as Killultagh. Unfortunately, we do not have detailed contemporary descriptions of these woods, but a number of documents refer to their extent and provide some indication of their importance. These sources generally support the map information, as they suggest that the main woods in this region were in the land known as the Dufferin in mid-Down and in Killultagh.[2]

Looking more closely at the landscape around Belfast Lough, a map of around 1570 attributed to Robert Lythe shows woodland mainly comprised of spaced trees below Cave Hill and a much more extensive area of dense woodland along the Lagan and nearby streams. This map does not distinguish between tall trees and underwood, but does include an annotation which refers to the Lagan Valley woods.

> *Along this River bi ye space of 26 miles groweth muche woods, as well okes for timber as hothar woodde wiche maie be brought in the baie of Cragfargus, with bote or by drage.*[3]

The mention of oak large enough to warrant being transported 'with bote or by drage' suggests that Francis Jobson's description of the Lagan Valley woods was perhaps over-simplistic. Oak was probably not the only tall tree present, but was specifically mentioned as it was the most important timber for building and many other uses.

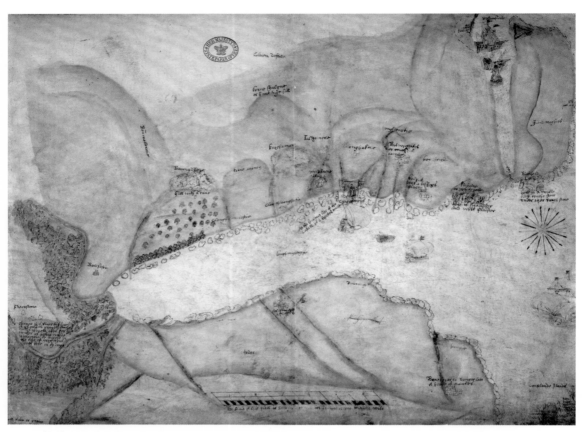

Map of Belfast Lough attributed to Robert Lythe. The annotation refering to trees is on the left hand side of the map, by the wooded Lagan.

The map evidence for a contrast between a wooded landscape around Belfast and more open conditions near Carrickfergus is supported by a number of documents from the second half of the 16th century which indicate that the people of Carrickfergus went to Belfast to obtain wood for fires and larger pieces of timber for building.[4] Evidence that there was still woodland in the northern Lagan Valley towards the end of the century is suggested by a statement by the Constable of Carrickfergus in 1591 that 'it is desirable to retain certain places in the Queen's possession, as the Castle of Belfast, which is environed with woods, whence (throughout this country) most mischiefs do spring.'[5]

By the beginning of the 17th century, British influence was growing throughout the region. A key figure was Sir Arthur Chichester, who arrived in Ireland in 1599 and by 1603 had been appointed governor of Carrickfergus and granted, for him and his heirs, Belfast Castle and 55 townlands in south Antrim, including what is now south, west and north Belfast. Shortly afterwards he was appointed Lord Deputy of Ireland.[6]

Amongst the correspondence of Sir Arthur Chichester is a letter of 1608 in which he described the woods around his new estate. Although the language and spelling make the letter quite difficult to follow, it does confirm what we know from other sources about the distribution of woods in the region between Knockfergus (Carrickfergus) and Killultagh. The letter also suggests that Chichester was aware that the woodland resource was limited but that rather than protecting the remaining trees his interest was in determining how they might be removed to provide timber.

> *...about Knockfergus there are no woods neere than Belfast wc is eight myles off but lyenge upon the river wh is portable, I have ther some wooken [oaken] trees but so crooked & shrofed [shrubbed] that no man fells them for tymber either for pipestaves or other use of buyldinge, but it maye be they wyll serve for some use for shippinge, such as they are....Kylultagh lyes on the one syde upon loage Eagh [Lough Neagh] & on the other syde upon the river of the lagan wh is the river that*

16

*runes by Belfast to Knockfergus, in that countrie are good tymber trees, but the countrie is but small, & therfore the quantitie
of tymber can not be great, this belonges to Sir Foulke Conwaye & as I conceive a small charge wyll clense that river…as
to make it portable of tymbers…*[7]

By 1611 Chichester had started to develop Belfast and a new brick castle was constructed on the remains of
the old O'Neill fortification. This castle was situated in what is now the centre of Belfast and just to the north
a planned town was laid out in the area around Waring Street (formerly Broad Street) and High Street.

Some indication of the conditions in which the residents lived in the 17th century can be gleaned from
orders made by the Assembly and entered into the Town Book of Belfast. For example, butchers had to
dispose of the remains of cattle at sea because of complaints that 'by killing and slaughtering of Catle they
suffer the Blood and Garbage of their slaughter houses, some to lye in ye streets & other parte to run into
severall channells and ditches of this Towne to the corruption and putrefaccon of the River and anoyance
of their neighbours by reason of the stinke and evill and infectious smell'. The occupiers of buildings and
land fronting onto streets or lanes also had to clean their portion of the street twice weekly (on Wednesday
and Saturday). Problems of flooding are suggested by a declaration of the Assembly that the inhabitants
had to build up sections of the banks of the river with brick or stone and lime to the same height as the
river wall. To improve security and visibility from 29 September to 25 March inhabitants in every street
and lane had to hang out 'one Lanthorne and candle lighted from ye houre of seaven oClock till ten at
night when it is not moon-shine'.[8]

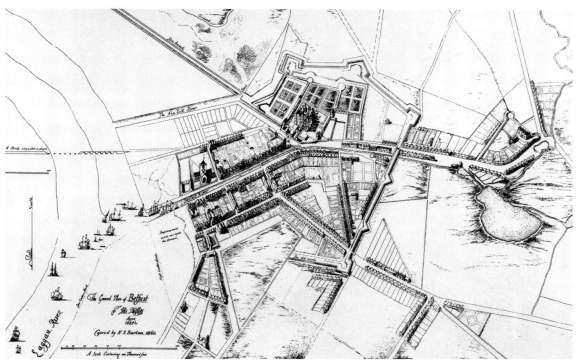

*Ground Plan of Belfast, 1685. Contrary to modern convention, the north arrow points downwards. Towards the top of the map can be
seen Belfast Castle and formal gardens within the ramparts.*

Brief descriptions of Belfast Castle and its gardens suggest a more pleasant environment. Sir William
Brereton in his travels in Ireland in 1635 visited Belfast Castle, which he thought was a 'dainty stately
house', and noted that an outer brick wall was being built around it. He described the grounds as having
orchards, gardens and walks that extended to the lough. This landscape changed when in 1642 earth
ramparts were built by the castle as part of the town defences. Later the bank by the castle became a
garden feature; around 1666 payment was made for 'making Boarders [Borders] at the Rampier, and for
women gathering Violats in ye Fields to sett in the Gardens.' Gardens were developed south of the castle
where they merged with demesne lands and in 1698 were described as being 'very spacious, with every
variety of walks, both close and open, fish ponds and groves'.[9]

The northern Lagan Valley

The eastern bank of the River Lagan was, at the beginning of the 17th century, part of the north Down lordship of Con O'Neill. However, the expansion of English power resulted in Con O'Neill disposing of townland after townland. One of these was Ballynafeigh, across the river from Belfast Castle. A deed dating from 1610 concerning this townland is of particular interest as it refers to woodland management. Land was leased to a tanner and carpenter who were not to use timber to burn bricks or tiles without licence and woods thought fit for barking were not to be felled before 1st May, so that the bark could be used for tanning. The tenants had to maintain the 'springs' and 'coppyis' (regrowth of underwood and/or coppice trees). Wood for firing, hedging and fencing was reserved for the use of the owner of the land.[10] It is possible that the trees at Ballynafeigh were part of a larger area of managed underwood or coppice woodland, as the beautiful 1625 maps of north Down drawn by Thomas Raven show land nearby, at Ballyhackamore and Ballymacarrett, as 'shrub wood'.[11]

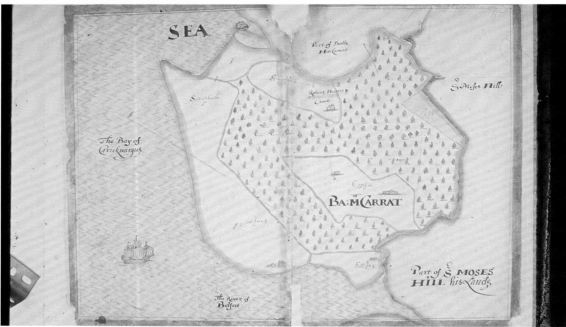

Raven maps of Ballyhackamore and Ballymacarrett.

Further south along the eastern bank of the Lagan lay the early church of Breda, in land now known as Belvoir Park. Recent research has provided remarkable insights into the early history and landscape of this district. Tree ring dating has identified some oak trees that are exceptionally old, with the oldest dating from 1642.[12] It is likely that these were not isolated trees and that in the mid 17th century there was woodland with oak trees, remnants of which have survived to the present day.

On the western bank of the Lagan, to the south of the castle and its gardens and meadows, was a district known as Cromock, now Cromac, part of Lower Ormeau. This area was wooded, in 1666 payment was made for 'cutting and binding 4000 Faggots in Crummuck Wood'[13] (a faggot was a term used for a bundle of sticks around 3 feet long and 2 feet in girth). Cromac occupied low lying land on the banks of the Blackstaff and Lagan Rivers and may well have periodically flooded. However, this was unlikely to have been an unwanted wasteland but rather a valuable and managed resource watched over by staff at the adjacent castle.

To the south, on higher well-drained land, was the area of Friar's Bush (today the name of the burial ground by the Botanic Gardens) and Malone, which was known as 'the Plains' suggesting open ground with few trees. Further upstream, land near the Lagan at Stranmillis was leased to a settler called Moyses Hill around the beginning of the century but at the end of the lease, in 1667, the land reverted to the Chichester family, who by then were known by their title of Donegall.[14]

A document of 1670 listing lands of the Earl of Donegall referred to these areas as 'the Demesnes of Strandmellis Cromock and Fryors Bush'.[15] Demesnes were lands held by the manor for its own use and purposes and in Belfast the demesne lands extended southwards from the castle gardens and included a continuous belt of land to Stranmillis. The 1670 document also noted that 'one hundred acres are now enclosed in a Deerepark with Pales and called Strandmellis Parke'. Deer parks were often created at a distance from the main house and Stranmillis would have been chosen because it fulfilled the main requirements for such an undertaking, with meadowland, woodland, a good water supply and a site that could be easily enclosed. Pales were a type of wooden deer fence traditionally made from cleft oak posts set vertically and fixed to a horizontal rail.

There was a plan to fence the rest of the demesne[15] though a description of the region from 1683 seems to only mention the park at Stranmillis, noting that on the right hand side of the road from Lisburn to Belfast 'the Countess of Donegall hath a very fine Park well stored with venison, and in it a horse course of two miles'. The horse course is thought to have followed the boundary of the deer park, a tear-drop shape formed by what are now the Stranmillis and Malone Roads, an area that was still referred to as 'the Course' in the 18th century.[16]

Other enclosed parks near Belfast

Castle Robin
In the Lagan Valley to the southwest of the Donegall lands lay the Conway Estate, and in a letter in the State Papers from 1628 we read that Lord Conway was 'anxious to have a park' and was enquiring about the cost of paling.[17] Two years later a man called Symon Richardson set out options for creating this park near Lisnagarvy (Lisburn):

> *Advantages of Lawrie's land, on the side of the hill against Castle Robbin: It is a light dry piece of ground, better for riding and coursing than the low ground near the town of Lisnagarvy. Part of it is limestony, and would be good for a sheep-walk, whilst another part is hard and with a fine view, which would produce hard-hoofed and 'cheerful and well-breathed' horses.*
> *Its disadvantages: It is some way from his Lordship's chief house, and would really only be useful for game and horse-breeding. It has woods at the bottom which must be taken in, but are hard to drain, and it is not altogether free from highways.*
> *Advantages of the ground next the town: It is rich land, has no highway and is near the lord's chief house, and is well wooded. The wood by careful management and by pollarding the old trees would supply the lord with timber and firewood for ever. The woods may easily be preserved and made most useful, but if they are not controlled they will run to waste and havoc and the lord will be compelled to use turf ('a bad kind of fuel') or get his wood from far.[18]*

This remarkable correspondence provides an insight into the planning that went into the development of this and probably other sites. It also contains some interesting comments about trees that show that the writer appreciated the desirability of woodland management. The reference to pollarding (where the upper branches of trees, above the trunk, are regularly cut to produce a crop of wood) is also fascinating as this is not thought to have been a common practice in Ireland. Pollarding would, however, have been useful in a deer park as the new growth sprouting from the top of the trunk would have been too high for deer to graze.

Correspondence from later in 1630 refers to the post and rail for the park being ready for erection from 'lying and dotard [decayed] timber'.[19] Maintenance of fencing was a major cost for parks and this use of cheap materials was probably a false economy that only provided a short-term solution. A list of payments made in 1665 included expenditure for mending the pales at Castle Robin Park, and in this year it was proposed to use income received from grazing at Castle Robin to pay for building a stone wall to surround the park.[20] However, in 1670 the park was emptied. It had been stocked with deer and the majority (more than 100 brace) were taken to a park created at Portmore on the south eastern shore of Lough Neagh. Some went to other sites, including 10 brace (20 animals) for Lord Donegall.[21]

Enclosing the Deer Park, Cave Hill. An historical illustration drawn in 1895 by J.W. Carey.

Oldpark
A report of around 1611 referred to an enclosed park three miles in circumference created in north Belfast by Arthur Chichester.

> Not farr from Bealfast the said Sr Arthure Chichester hath impalled a parke of three myle Compasse where he intendes to buyld a house of Lyme and stone, but a tymber house wth chimneys is already buylte therin, which is Compassed about with a Rampier of earth and soddes and a deepe ditch standinge full of water in wch house there nowe dwelleth one Liutent [Lieutenant] Lowsley with his famelie.[22]

By 1670 it had become known as the Old Park, perhaps because it was no longer in use. However, there may have been an attempt to create a second park in the area, as leases refer to 125 acres called the New Enclosures that were bounded in part by the townland of Skegoneill and 'the lands called the old parke'.[23]

The name New Enclosures (sometimes spelt Inclosures) suggests that this land may have been at one time surrounded by a pale, though no documentary evidence for this has been found. We have no other information about this park and its surroundings, with the exception of a reference in a lease for the area of 1688 to 'that parcel of land commonly called Mankin's copse containing by estimation twenty acres of land more or less'.[24] It is not known exactly where this land was situated though the mention of a copse (a thicket of trees, often coppiced) is of interest. Today, the only link we have to the early landscape of north Belfast is the name of the site, Oldpark, now a suburb of the city.

The New Parke on Cave Hill

An area near Belfast called the New Parke is mentioned in a census of Ireland dating from around 1659 and again in a listing of the Donegall estate lands of 1670 which refers to the New Parke as comprising 'one halfe of the Towne land of Listilliard and part of Clough Castle', lands in the vicinity of Cave Hill.[25] The date of the formation of the park is not known, though George Benn, author of *A History of the Town of Belfast* (1877, 1880), referred to an oral tradition that the first Earl of Donegall enclosed the Cave Hill Park by a wall around 1666.[26] This was to be the longest lasting deer park in the Belfast area, and its development is described in the next chapter.

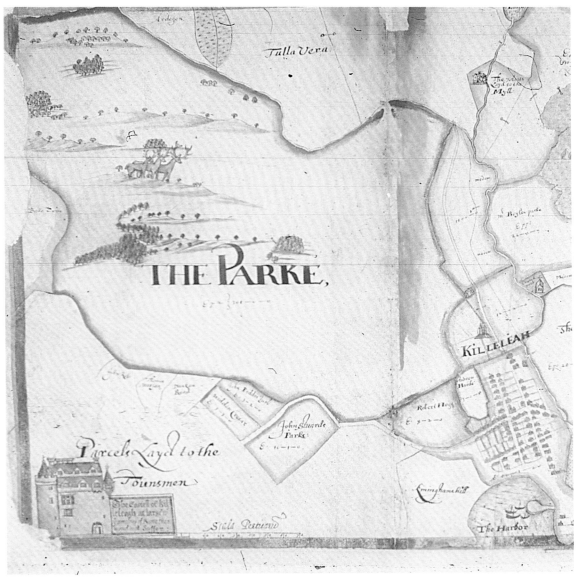

This map of Killyleagh, County Down by Thomas Raven of 1625 provides a beautiful illustration of a deer park.

Tree felling

It is likely that trees were managed in demesne lands, deer parks and at some woodlands. However at other sites trees were undoubtedly felled at an ever-increasing rate to meet the needs of the expanding communities centred on Belfast and Carrickfergus. The fear of men hiding in woods, including those that the newcomers had dispossessed, may well also have encouraged clearance. Brief descriptions of the landscape around Belfast in the mid 17th century suggest that by this time much of the woodland in the northern Lagan Valley had been cleared and a pastoral landscape created. For example, William Brereton in his account of his travels in 1635 described the route from Belfast to Lisburn as 'a paradise in comparison of any part of Scotland' and the Franciscan Father MacCana who visited Belfast around 1644 found the lands on either side of the River Lagan 'pleasant and fertile'. The Civil Survey boundary description of 1654-56 for the barony of Castlereagh (southeast of Belfast) referred to bogs, heath, pasture and tillage and added that 'in this barony are few woods left', a statement that indicates clearance.[27] A picture of the landscape towards the end of the century is provided by a document of 1692 that briefly lists Donegall lands. 5,000 acres was described as pasture and 1,000 acres each of meadow, moor, marsh, wood and underwood, furze and heath. An additional 100 acres was described as rushes and 100 acres as alder-wood.[28]

An indication of the extent of tree felling is shown by an agreement between Con O'Neill and Hugh Montgomery of 1606 concerning the timber and mining rights over a region of northwest County Down called Slutt McNeale or the Kellyes Country. Montgomery was allowed to cut, dress and transport timber using the river, land or sea and to remain on the land and construct buildings for security. Tenants were allowed to cut trees (except oak) for their own buildings though the waste of timber was forbidden and any offender might be called before Montgomery's court. Montgomery was also allowed to graze hogs in the woods. There is a noticeable absence of any mention of replanting or to the protection of trees, though what was described as the wood of Castlereagh Demesne was excluded from the agreement.[29]

Timber was used for building work, for use around the farm and for a variety of industries, including charcoal-making for ironworks which developed in the northern Lagan Valley at Ardoyne, Stranmillis, Lambeg, Newforge and Oldforge.[30] The ironworks at Stranmillis was established in 1612, the lease entitling wood to be taken from Chichester's land at Malone and Falls (on the County Antrim side of the River Lagan) and in the following year a lease was signed with Hugh Montgomery to cut wood in 60 townlands in what had been O'Neill's land on the County Down side of the river.[31] The ironworks at Newforge was also a large-scale operation: it was reported that 1,000 tons of square timber and 1,000 loads of charcoal were lost when the site was destroyed in the 1641 Rebellion. It is likely that trees across the River Lagan at Belvoir Park were cut to supply Newforge. Evidence to support this is suggested by recent tree dating at Belvoir, which found that the oldest oak started to grow in 1642, a year after the Newforge ironworks were destroyed and timber cutting would have ceased.[32] Most ironworks seem to have been short-lived operations that made use of the local timber resource and when this was exhausted a new site was chosen.[33] This could be seen as an unsustainable exploitation of woodland by new landowners who were only interested in quick profits, though there is evidence that, at least in some instances, ironworks were encouraged for the purpose of clearing scrub to create agricultural land.[34]

Farming would have had a particularly significant impact on reducing woodland cover. Leases from the second half of the 17th century for the Brownlow Estate in north Armagh indicate that tenants were sometimes required to clear the land of scrub and bushes. The importance given to clearing the land was underscored by the inclusion in some leases of a timescale for this work. Once trees had been removed, grazing and ploughing would have prevented regeneration. In the early Brownlow leases tenants were permitted wood for building, fencing and firewood though from the 1680s onwards the provision of free timber was restricted. These late 17th century leases also sometimes referred to saplings (particularly of oak) that had to be pruned and preserved, conditions that were overseen by a wood ranger.[35] This change in emphasis suggests that, as a result of clearance, trees were soon not seen simply as an impediment to agriculture, but as a dwindling resource that needed to be managed.

Tree planting

While woods and areas of scrub were being cleared, some trees were being planted. Although this tree planting probably had a negligible impact on the overall level of tree cover, it would have helped create new landscapes. In particular, hedges started to become common around Belfast during the 17th century, planted by settlers who introduced new farming methods and desired to mark out land boundaries. A document of 1610 concerning the colonisation of Ulster referred to the planting of quicksets (quicks being young hedging trees). It was proposed that 'four years for building a castle, storehouse, or bawne, is the least time that may be allowed them; within which time it is necessary that they be enjoined to enclose with strong ditches and quickset a meet proportion of their land after the manner of England.'[36] A report of around 1611 into the work undertaken in the Belfast area included a good description of just such a property near Knockfargus (Carrickfergus) which it seems used hedges both for defence and to enclose fields.

> A myle and somewhat more from Knockfargus we sawe a farme house of the Lo: Deputies buylte of Tymber after the English fashion inclosed rounde with a bawne, ditched aboute, and a stronge hedge thereupon...There are many Inclosiers neere the said house neewly made, with good ditches, sett with wyllowes and a great parte with quicksetts, where his Lop hath nowe a stocke of English Cowes, Sheepe, and other Cattell.[37]

The planting of tall, forest trees was quite often stipulated in leases of this period. Generally these trees were to be planted along hedges. For example, in Ballinderry near Lisburn in 1653 tenants had to plant ten young trees of oak or ash every year on a double ditch 'in such manner as they may grow for the benefit of the landlord and his heirs.'[38] At the Brownlow Estate there was similarly a requirement to plant hawthorn hedges that included tall growing trees (sycamore, ash or oak).[39] Sometimes more general tree planting as well as hedge planting was stipulated, though, given the size of the areas leased, the numbers of trees to be planted tended to be small. An indenture between Arthur, Earl of Donegall and Thomas Waring of 1659 for all of the townland of Skegoneill and quarter of the adjoining townland of Listillyard included a condition to plant on this land just 500 young oak, ash or elm trees.[40] Two leases of land by the

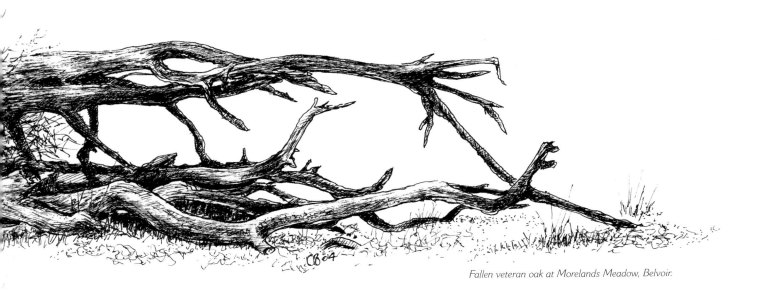

Fallen veteran oak at Morelands Meadow, Belvoir.

CRANMORE near BELFAST.

Drawn on Stone by A. McQuilian *From a Drawing by E. M.*

Engraving of Cranmore published in 1853.

Countess of Longford in north Belfast dating from 1691 had requirements to plant and preserve 'on some convenient part of the premises' young oak, ash, elm or beech trees as well as planting any fences or enclosures with hedges. In one of these leases of 23 acres the tenant had to plant 92 trees and in the other lease of 125 acres the tenant was instructed to plant 500 trees.[41] In both instances this equates to planting four trees per acre.

By the second half of the 17th century orchards were being widely planted; the road from Lambeg to Belfast was described at this time as 'all along for the most part furnished with houses, little orchards, and gardens'.[42] Some leases for the Brownlow Estate stipulated the planting of small mixed orchards that would provide apples, pears, plums and also cherries.[43] Judging from the correspondence of Major George Rawdon, agent to Viscount Conway, one reason for the popularity of orchards was the value of the fruit in making alcoholic beverages. For example, in one letter of 1664 Rawdon wrote that 'The object of the orchard is chiefly to make cyder. I wish your lordship could find us some young trees of that naughty apple only fit for that use. I have forgot its name.'[44]

Other correspondence for the Conway Estate suggests that a desire to improve orchards may have been significant in starting the importation of trees into the region. In 1665, a letter from Adam Leathes at Lisburn to Viscount Conway mentioned that 'the gardener wants some pear kirnells sent over to sow for raising stocks to graft upon.' Two years later, George Rawdon wrote of apple trees being 'brought over' and requested that shoots (scions) for grafting onto apple root stock be sent. Subsequently he reported his annoyance that, although a batch of scions had arrived in time, 'the labels, being of paper, were rotted off, and we have had to guess at the various sorts'. In 1669, Rawdon wrote of the arrival of French seed and of unnamed trees from Bordeaux.[45]

The earliest example of the large scale planting of ornamental exotic trees in the Belfast region was by Rawdon's son, Sir Arthur Rawdon, at Moira. Here, from the 1680s until his death in 1695, Arthur Rawdon assembled an impressive collection of plants during a period of great political turmoil. In this task he was aided by his friendship with Sir Hans Sloane of Killyleagh, a naturalist who visited Jamaica as physician to the governor. Rawdon received seeds from Sloan and plants from the Chelsea Physic Garden. He commissioned James Harlow (a gardener who had previously collected for the Chelsea garden), to travel to Jamaica to obtain plants. Harlow returned in 1692, landing at Carrickfergus with twenty cases,

24

Cranmore and the two remaining sweet chestnut trees in 2008.

each containing about 50 shrubs and trees, together with ferns, a few herbaceous plants and seeds.[46] It is likely that other landowners around Belfast were importing and planting ornamental trees by the second half of the 17th century. One line of evidence for this is provided by early references to large non-native trees. For example, in the papers of the Ward Family of County Down there is a letter of 1725 about their property at Bangor which mentions a walnut tree 'whos trunke is 10 feet long and almoste 6 feet about at 5 feet high.'[47] This tree must have been planted in the 17th century. Similarly, John Dubourdieu, the author of *The Statistical Survey of the County of Antrim* published in 1812, identified a few exotic trees that, from their size, he thought had been planted before 1700. These were some old walnut trees in the village of Lambeg and a row of sweet chestnut trees planted in front of the 17th century house known as Orange Grove (later called Cranmore) on the Malone Road. Remarkably, two of these sweet chestnut trees still stand by the now roofless shell of Cranmore house. These may be the oldest garden trees that are today growing in Belfast.[48]

Measurements of the Cranmore sweet chestnut trees.

	Southern tree	Middle tree	Northern tree
John Templeton in 1807 Measured at breast height	11 feet 10 inches (3.60m)	6 feet 8 inches (2.03m)	9 feet 6½ inches (2.89m)
John Dubourdieu in 1811 Measured at 4 foot	12 feet (3.65m)	6 feet 10 inches (2.08m)	9 feet 11 inches (3.02m)
Mrs Templeton, quoted in 1838 Measured at 1 foot	15 feet (4.57m)		
Douglas Deane in 1979 Measured at breast height	21 feet 10 inches (6.66m)		
Ben Simon in 2005 Southern tree measured at 1.5m, middle tree at 1.7m	25 feet 2 inches (7.67m)	14 feet 2 inches (4.32m)	Gone

These are the only trees in the Belfast region that have been repeatedly measured over a long period of time. The northern tree, which had a crooked stem, most likely fell sometime before 1945 when a brief description of the site only referred to two sweet chestnut trees. Today all that remains of this tree is a few decaying pieces of the trunk.[49]

3. Trees in a developing town
1700-1800

The Donegall Estate lands

Accounts listing payments and receipts for the Donegall Estate for the first few years of the 18th century suggest that life for Belfast's foremost family was continuing much as before. In 1706 there was routine maintenance on Belfast Castle with payment for 'slating and pointing and severall other particulars' and in this year the upkeep of the gardens included 16s 4d for '28 days work repairing the dark walk in ye Castle Garden.' Another payment of 6d to a man called Thomas Glass 'for nails for the boxes of the trees in the street' suggests that at this time street trees were being grown in ornamental planters to enhance Belfast. The listing of expenditure for 1706 also included a cost for bringing hawks from Inishowen, which was part of the Donegall Estate. Hawks would have been high status animals and there are references to payments (again to Thomas Glass) for providing meat for the hawks and a lovely note detailing the expenditure of 2d 'for pack thread for ye Hawkes Creels which went to Mallahyde.'[1]

However, life for the Donegalls was to change forever when in 1706 the third Earl of Donegall was killed during a battle in Spain. Two years later there was a second disaster for the family when Belfast Castle was accidentally burned and three daughters of the late Earl were amongst those who perished in the blaze. The family subsequently moved to England and, as the fourth Earl was of weak intellect, the estate was placed under trustees until his death in 1757.[2]

In the years following the fire, the estate accounts refer to the dismantlement of the castle remains. In 1709 payment was made for taking down battlements on top of the castle wall. In 1713 income was received for lead 'gathered from amongst the rubbish of the Castle'. In 1714 labourers were paid for pulling down the old wall of the castle and cleaning and piling the bricks, some of which were sold the following year.[3] In 1716 the outbuildings together with some gardens and meadows were leased, though it was stipulated that the lease would be terminated if the family decided to repair or rebuild the castle. This idea seems to have been quickly abandoned, as in 1717 there was a further lease of lands near the former castle and the extensive demesnes.[4]

Although it could be imagined that by this stage the Donegall family would have had little direct involvement in the affairs of Belfast, surviving account books indicate that the family retained an interest in some sites. The information is fragmentary but includes many references to the Belfast Castle gardens, Cromac Wood and the Cave Hill Deer Park.

Belfast Castle gardens
In the years after the castle fire, items listed under income include the sale of a few trees in the castle gardens. All of these trees are described as wind-blown, dead or decayed, evidence that although the

South Belfast including Castle Meadows, Town Parks, Cromac Wood and the Course Lands
from the Donegall Estate maps of 1767-1770 by James Crow.

27

castle had gone the gardens were not a derelict site to be cleared of trees but remained an actively managed landscape.[5]

We know little about the appearance of the area in the following decades, though vouchers for payments made in the 1730s and 1740s refer to money being spent on the maintenance and improvement of the walls, castle court and gate. Also, although the Donegall family was not resident, there were regular payments for the upkeep of a building in the area that was called Lord Donegall's house. Repairs to this house (including a substantial rebuilding in 1741) indicate that it was an old structure, perhaps an outbuilding that had escaped the fire. Later in the century this was the rent office and residence of the Donegall's agent and became known, like its much grander predecessor, as 'the Castle.'[6]

1712	15 decayed Trees sold out of the Grove in the Castle Garden of Belfast	£2 10s
1713	an old dead tree in the Grove in the Castle Garden	4s
1714	two Ash Trees which were Blown down in the Castle Garden of Belfast	£1 4s
1714	4 ash trees as aforesaid	£1 1s 8d
1715	a small Sycomer [sycamore] Tree broke by the wind in the Castle Garden of Belfast	4s 4d

Income from the sale of timber from the castle gardens.[5]

The gardens were still an attractive managed landscape when Richard Pococke, Bishop of Meath, visited the area during his tour of Ireland in 1752. He was unimpressed by Belfast, which he described as comprising 'of one long broad Street, and of several lanes in which the inferior people live'. In contrast his visit to the grounds by the former castle prompted him to write that 'the garden, groves, meadows and fields on the river…are very delightful.'[7] An enclosed space around the site of the castle was to remain as late as 1782 when an advertisement appeared for the lease of 'the Gardens commonly known by the name of the Castle Garden' described as an eight-acre site in three distinct enclosures.[8]

In 1784 plans were put in place to redevelop the area.[9] Donegall Place was laid out and a new focal point was provided with the building of Belfast's White Linen Hall (which would eventually be levelled to provide the site for the present City Hall). It is perhaps fitting that the last link we have to the historic landscape around the castle are references to trees. In March 1784 trees in front of the Linen Hall, described as very fine birch, elm and ash, were auctioned. Six months later there was a further sale of trees that were presumably quite old as they were removed because they were shading the windows at the front of the new Linen Hall. In 1795 there was a final auction of 16 elm and 10 ash trees growing by the nearby Mall.[10]

Cromac Wood

The earliest detailed maps of Cromac Wood show six wide avenues that converged on a central point. These were said to have been created by the third Earl of Donegall to provide access for the people of Belfast for recreation[11] and were known as 'passes' (a pass was a word used to describe a route cut through a wood). The passes were also undoubtedly used to improve access for grazing and timber extraction.

According to the historian Colin Johnston Robb, the third Earl stocked Cromac Wood with pheasants and appointed as keeper a man called James Bickerstaff.[12] The earliest detailed information relating to Cromac Wood, however, refers not to management for game birds but to grazing and cutting. For example, the Donegall accounts of 1706 list income for 'graseing in Crumoak' and in 1711 itemise '1100 faggots at 5s 6d p hundred which were cutt out of the Passes of Crumoak Wood.'[13] Historically, there was a distinction made between small diameter material (known as wood) that might be bound together to make faggots and bigger diameter material like tree trunks (known as timber) that could be used to make planks and beams. The item of expenditure of £1 2s 9d in 1739 claimed by a man called Francis Cowell 'for his trouble in selling Lord Donegall's timber in Crumock'[14] is therefore of interest as it suggests that tall trees as well as scrub and branches were being cut at Cromac.

View of Belfast from Cromac Wood by Jonathan Fisher, 1772.

Occasional advertisements from the 1750s to 1780s for grazing[15] and for cows and horses having strayed or been stolen from Cromac Wood[16] indicate that the area must by this stage have included grasslands. Further insights into the development of the landscape are provided by leases for Cromac dating from 1770. The leaseholders were permitted to 'grub up, take away and convert to his and their own use all the Underwood or Brushwood now growing on the premises….Except and always reserved out of this present Demise unto the said Earl…all manner of Timber and other Trees Saplings and Standils [young trees reserved for timber production] growing or hereafter to grow on the said demised premises'. The leases also stated that the reserved timber trees had to be 'effectively preserved from destruction and damage by cattle'.[17] This kind of land management, where some trees are protected but scrub is removed and the land is grazed, would have prevented natural regeneration and resulted in Cromac Wood becoming parkland with spaced, mature trees and meadows.

There may have been a deliberate plan to change Cromac Wood from woodland to farmland. In 1773 an advertisement was placed for 'grazing for a few Cattle to be had in a Quarter of the Wood which is cleared', land which was said to have plenty of grass.[18] This had been a southern section of the wood and in April 1786 the clearance of the main part of Cromac Wood was announced when the Belfast News-Letter advertised the sale of the timber trees, principally oak with some ash and alder. A later advertisement noted that the oak trees of Cromac Wood were to be sold 'as they now lie', suggesting that they were of a substantial size.[19]

A map of Belfast from 1791 shows a few big trees still standing at Cromac, mainly along hedge lines.[20] However, much of the landscape had changed forever and a contemporary advertisement for Cromack Wood Farm stated that the agricultural value of the land had been improved and was now mostly meadows.[21] In 1792 a visitor to Belfast wrote that 'A great wood has been recently cut down close to the public walk [the Mall] at Belfast' and when George Benn published *The History of the Town of Belfast* in 1823 all that was recalled was that Cromac had been principally an oak wood and the haunt of swans.[22]

deliver Lime on very moderate terms at any convenient landing place in either the county of Down or Antrim.

Gentlemen who live nigh to the Loughs of Belfast or Strangford, will certainly find it their interest to be supplied with Lime from those Kilns.

Larne, 18th April, 1786.

To be Sold by Auction,

THE Timber Trees standing and growing in Cromack Wood, near Belfast; consisting principally of Oak, with some Ash and Alder;——to be set up in such Lots as shall be most agreeable to the purchasers.

The Sale to begin on Monday the eighth of May next, at eleven o'Clock Forenoon.

25th April, 1786.

To be Sold by public Auction,

At the Donegall-Arms in Belfast, on Monday the 22d day of May next, at twelve o'Clock at Noon;

A Lease of sundry Messuages or Tenements in Peters-

or cloth with him to take them away without loss of time lest they should be mislaid, and all is now ready.

Dated at Antrim, 9th August, 1786.

OAK TREES.

THE TREES in CRUMACK WOOD to be sold by Auction as they now lie, on Friday next the 18th inst. at one o'Clock at noon :——To be set up in such Lots as may be approved of by the Purchasers. Terms of payment by Bills on Dublin or this Town at three months date.

Belfast, 11th August, 1786.

Royal Sport of Cockfighting.

THERE will be a Main of thirty-one Stags and fifteen Byes shewn in the town of Moneymore, on Saturday the 26th instant, and be fought in said town

The second half of the 18th century also witnessed large-scale felling at two other long established woods in the Belfast region. At Glenarm there is reference to the felling of old oak trees, timber from this wood was said to have been used to build the brig *Shillelagh*, launched at Belfast in 1793.[23] At Killultagh (Portmore, near Lough Neagh) when Lord Conway's house was dismantled in 1761, the extensive woods were cleared over a 20-year period, timber sales fetching an average of £500 a year.[24]

Cave Hill Deer Park

Accounts for the Donegall Estate for the 18th century provide some fascinating details about the development and management of a deer park at Cave Hill. At the beginning of the century, in 1706, there was a small income received for grazing and a payment of £2 6s made to George Foster for work that included 'plowing ground in Cave Hill park'. This suggests that at this time deer were absent or only occupying part of the land, a view supported by a payment in 1709 to labourers for 'enclosing three acres & a halfe of meadow and making and stacking Hay for the Deer' and in 1710 for 'moeing [mowing] 3 acres & a halfe of Meadow for the Deer.' Reference in the following years to the employment of a park keeper and regular repairs to the boundaries suggest that the deer had been given the run of the park.[25]

We know that the Deer Park had both walls and wooden fencing (pales) as there are references to the building and repair of walls in 1708 at a cost of £28 5s 3d and in 1710 a carpenter received 2s to repair the pales of the Deer Park.[25] Over the years keeping the deer within the park proved to be very expensive. In 1714 Mr Green received two payments, of £100 and of £98 2s, on account of the Deer Park wall and £4 13s 3d for repairing fences of the Deer Park. In the following year there were again large payments for repairing the park wall and gates and there are records of the employment of masons and labourers in 1734, 1739 and 1741.[25,26] It is possible that the decay of the wall was exacerbated by vandalism: in 1766 a notice placed by the Earl of Donegall stated that the walls of the Deer Park had been 'frequently broke or pulled down by idle or designing People from the adjoining Mountain.'[27]

The first person recorded as park keeper was William Dumbill, who was paid £7 10s for a year and a quarter's wages in 1712.[28] Subsequent park keepers included George Ash and John Rice. John Rice was in post for a number of years at a salary of £10 per year[29] and we know a little about where he lived from payments for 'his house in Belfast Deer park' that included straw for the roof and the cost of employing a thatcher. We also know what he wore to work, as a perk of the job was a uniform. The tailor's bills for the park keeper itemise a coat, waistcoat and greatcoat (but not trousers or shoes, which John Rice presumably had to buy for himself). The livery was all in green cloth and made up with a large number of buttons, some of which must have been for decoration. The cost of the materials in 1735 was £3 2s 10d and to make up the clothes an extra 8s 6d.[30]

In contrast to the details we have about the park keeper, the Donegall Estate records contain surprisingly few references to the animals kept in the park. A single reference of 1741 to expenditure of £1 on hay for

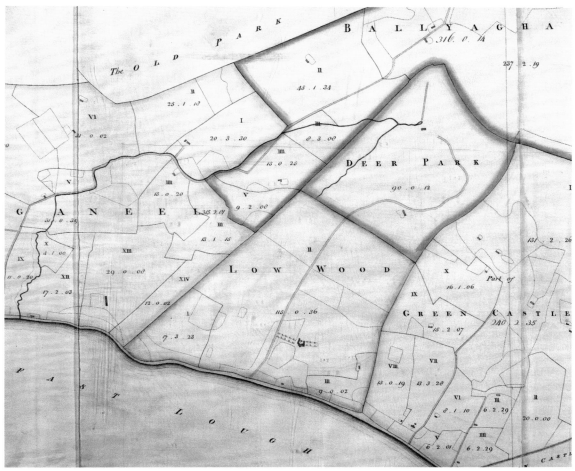

Cave Hill Deer Park. Detail from the Donegall Estate maps of 1767-1770 by James Crow.

the deer provides a glimpse into the management of the herd. This payment can be explained by the exceptional weather from 1739 to 1741 that included the winter known as the Great Frost. Another interesting note is an advertisement of 1795 for grazing to be let in the park. This may indicate that there were times when there were few if any deer kept at Cave Hill.[31]

Comments about trees at the Cave Hill Deer Park appear in a range of sources from the early, middle and latter parts of the 18th century. The earliest is in an account of a journey to the district by Thomas Molyneux in 1708:

> *We struck off from the Road, which runs all Long the Sea, to view a Park here belonging to the Lords of Donnegal. Here they carryed us up a pretty high Hill, where is a very pleasant Fountain, well shaded with Trees, and from whence you have a very fine Prospect of Carrickfergus, the Bay, and Belfast, which from hence makes a very good shew.[32]*

Estate records include two references to small-scale timber extraction, in 1735 a man was employed for two days at the Deer Park selling wind blown timber and subsequently Ralph Charly (Lord Donegall's bailiff) received 3s 6d for selling timber out of the park.[33] A short description of the Deer Park from 1778 refers to the park being 'walled in and covered with lofty trees, which adds greatly to its romantic appearance.' A painting of Belfast by John Nixon of around 1782 shows the area of the enclosure on Cave Hill as parkland, with large spaced trees.[34]

This landscape, however, changed dramatically when sometime near the end of the century the trees in the Deer Park were felled. This may have happened before 1790, when a short article about Belfast suggested that the natural beauties of Cave Hill might be enhanced if attention was paid to planting it. The trees were just a memory when George Benn wrote *The History of the Town of Belfast* (1823), though he provided a short comment in which he described them as having been a large plantation of old ash.[35]

Normally, when woods are felled, cut stumps sprout with new life and in the open conditions seedlings rapidly grow to form new trees. However, deer would have eaten young shoots and any saplings unless they were protected by fencing. The evidence provided by views of Cave Hill painted in the early 20th century suggests that there was no significant woodland regeneration. The once wooded slopes of Cave Hill Deer Park had almost overnight become open grassland.[36]

Wood rangers in the Donegall Estate

Information about the management of woods in Belfast at this time is sparse, though surviving 18th century records for the Donegall Estate do include a number of references to the employment of wood rangers (Appendix 1). We know that some of these men covered specific sites around Belfast, such as William Brown who was employed as wood ranger for Cromac Wood in the years 1739-1743. Occasionally invoices provide some evidence about their profession. Edward Fisher, a wood ranger between 1737 and 1740, received £1 in 1737 'for half a year's salary for taking care of his Lordships Timber in the Fall Mallone Dunmurry' and in the following year received £1 'for taking care of said Earls hedge roes in the Fall & Mallone'.[37]

Estate records and notices for the sale of woods from throughout Ireland in the 17th to 19th centuries quite often refer to wood rangers and in a brief survey of the literature references to a related profession of clerk of the woods have also been found.[38] Surprisingly, the roles played by these people have been almost completely ignored by commentators on Irish woods. An exception is to be found in an account of Ireland published by Edward Wakefield in 1812, though Wakefield unfortunately restricted his comments to a brief scathing attack. He noted that trees in Ireland were generally looked after either by farming stewards who knew little about plantations or by wood rangers who he considered 'the idlest and most drunken vagabonds in the kingdom.'[39] Leaving aside Wakefield's views, the fact that there was such a profession as wood ranger indicates that the care and protection of trees in estate lands was treated as a matter of some importance.

Two records relating to the protection of trees in Belfast also provide a fascinating glimpse into May Day folk traditions. These concern the payment of 1s 1d 'to the man who took Care of Crumoak Wood on May Day 1734' and a payment of 2s and 8½d in 1788 to 'John McGain & Partner watching the trees in & near the Mall to prevent their being topped for May-bushes.'[40] May Day had long been an important festival in Ireland and branches were cut to make a decorated May Bush, or a tree would be cut to make a May Pole. This was considered to be enough of a problem in the 18th century to warrant legislation to try to ban the practice and at Cromac Wood to employ men to keep guard over the trees.

The creation of new estates

By the 18th century a number of large estates were being developed around Belfast by wealthy tenants and landowners keen to promote their status. They generally followed a similar design, formed around a demesne with a large mansion house, pleasure grounds, a walled garden and a home farm.[41] The earlier estates, some of which can be traced back to the previous century, may have included formal landscapes, though by the mid 18th century the grounds around the big houses of Belfast were developed with the more naturalistic landscapes popular at this period. Creating these landscaped demesnes sometimes required roads and even settlements to be moved. High walls were constructed along road frontages and some demesnes, like deer parks, were completely surrounded by walls. Entrances were often marked by large gates and lodges. At Belvoir Park a substantial stone wall 5km long bounded the demesne on three sides, the fourth side being formed by the River Lagan and canal.[42] The adjacent demesne of Purdysburn was described in 1784 as being 'remarkably well enclosed'.[43] These barriers would have helped separate the idealised Arcadian landscapes of demesnes from the realities of the world outside and would have had a practical value in reinforcing ownership, deterring trespass and protecting property, trees and game.

Trees and woods contributed greatly to demesnes by creating impressive landscapes, highlighting views, acting as screens and forming a setting for the big house. Trees also provided firewood, timber and cover for game such as pheasants that were bred for shoots. Planting was sometimes on a large scale, such as at Castle Dobbs near Carrickfergus where, in 1739, Mr Dobbs was reported to have 'planted groves and

Detail from an illustration of Belfast from Friar's Bush by John Nixon c. 1782.
Widely spaced tall trees can be seen on the slopes above Belfast in the area of the Cave Hill Deer Park.

33

laid out avenues'.[44] Specimen trees were planted and in some estates non-native trees were used to great effect, such as at Bangor where it was noted that the mansion house was indifferent but that evergreen trees and shrubs were a notable feature.[45] We know from notices placed about theft and malicious damage that some demesnes were embellished with statuary; in one instance an irate landowner complained that a lead sculpture of Hercules with his club had been stolen from Purdysburn and on another occasion damage was done to a lead statue and sculptures of a rabbit and fox at Moira.[46] These ornaments were probably located in pleasure grounds near the mansion houses.

Belvoir Park was one of the largest demesnes to be created near Belfast. It can be traced back to the 1720s, when Arthur Hill first started to acquire land in the area. The earliest description found of Belvoir, published in 1740, refers to the grounds having been 'laid out lately in Taste' with gardens 'disposed in regular Canals, with Cascades, Slopes and Terraces, and the Kitchen Ground inclosed with Espaliers'. The 1740 account of Belvoir interestingly also noted that at this time the offices (outbuildings) had been finished but that the mansion was not yet built.[47]

The mansion house and demesne of Belvoir Park by Jonathan Fisher, c. 1770.

The formal landscaped gardens with espaliers (trained trees), canals (rectangular ponds) and terraces at Belvoir Park occupied a relatively small part of the demesne on either side of the River Lagan, close to where the house was to be constructed. The demesne also contained mature oak trees, areas of woodland managed for game and open land that was farmed. An important feature within the walled grounds was a wide ditch (a feature known as a ha-ha) to the east of the mansion house that separated the woodland and pleasure grounds near the house from an area where farm animals were grazed within hedged enclosures.[48]

The early history of the nearby Purdysburn Estate is poorly known. A document of 1712 mentions 'James Willson of Purdysburne', though the first reference found to improvements is in a brief note about the estate published in 1740. Development at this time is also suggested by a decorative stone at a summer house in the old walled garden which is carved 1740 and one large fallen oak tree, near the ice house in

Previous page: Belfast and the Lagan Valley from Belvoir Park by Jonathan Fisher c. 1770.
The well-wooded demesne in the foreground contrasts with the fields and hedges of the Lagan Valley.

Veteran oak in Purdysburn Demesne. This tree has a girth of 4.26m at 1.5 m.

the grounds, which recent tree ring dating has shown started to grow in 1737. This building and landscaping was most likely the work of Hill Willson, who inherited the estate from his father James in 1741.[49] A feature of the walled garden at Purdysburn was yew hedging said to have been laid out in the shape of the Union Jack. This may have been created in the 18th century.[50]

Notes written for a valuation of woods at Purdysburn list broadleaved species including woods of ash, oak and alder near the house and stream, hedgerows with ash trees and elsewhere elm, birch, sycamore and hazel.[51] A recent survey has shed some additional light on the early history of the demesne with the identification of a number of large circumference trees (mainly oak, beech and sycamore, see Appendix 4). They were planted to create parkland near the mansion house and probably date from the 18th century. In contrast to this open landscape, the demesne includes a valley, Purdysburn Glen, which has most likely long been kept as woodland.[52]

A third early Lagan Valley demesne was Malone, a property near Shaw's Bridge that is now the public park known as Barnett Demesne. The estate was the home of the Legg (or Legge) family who are thought to have leased the land from about 1665.[53] The earliest detailed information we have of this property is a fascinating map of the grounds of c.1780 that shows a patchwork of fields bounded by hedges planted with spaced tall trees. There were orchards and some woodlands and by the mansion house a kitchen garden and haggard (stackyard). Surprisingly there is no evidence of pleasure gardens, with the exception of a small area between the main road and house described as the front court and lawn.[54] The only ornamentation we know of concerns the planting of trees and flowering shrubs along walls adjoining Malone House in 1782.[55]

The fashion for creating and planting demesnes continued throughout the century. In 1744 it was noted that work at Orangefield in east Belfast had started the year before and that here 'Mr. Hunter has laid out also Gardens, Orchards, Lawns and other improvements suitable to the House'.[56] Wilmont (now Sir Thomas and Lady Dixon Park) is thought to have been founded in the early 1760s, and two oak stumps in the grounds that have been tree ring dated provide very similar start dates of 1775 and 1777, suggesting a period of planting shortly after of the creation of the demesne.[57]

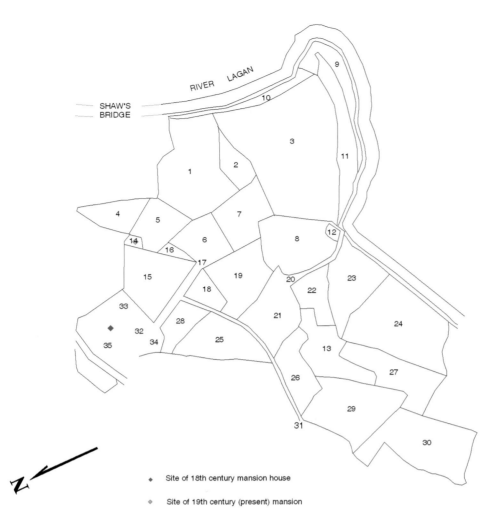

SHAW'S
BRIDGE

RIVER LAGAN

1 Mercers Field
2 Diers Field
3 Islands
4 Fir Grove
5 Christys Field
6 Springwell Field
7 Lower Springwell Field
8 Haystack Hill
9 Island Hoam
10 A Bank on the Canal
11 Island Wood
12 Dark Walk
13 Nursery Wood
14 A Moat in the Orchard
15 Orchard
16 Stripe
17 A Lane
18 Murays Field
19 Barrs Acre
20 A Lane
21 Lime Kiln Field
22 Fox Hole Hill
23 Old Green Hoam
24 Old Green Meadow
25 Brick Field Meadow
26 Fallow Field
27 Beef Park
28 Brick Field
29 Forth Field
30 Nellys Field
31 A Lane
32 Back Court etc
33 Kitchen Garden
34 Hagard
35 Front Court and Lawn

N

♦   Site of 18th century mansion house

◆   Site of 19th century (present) mansion

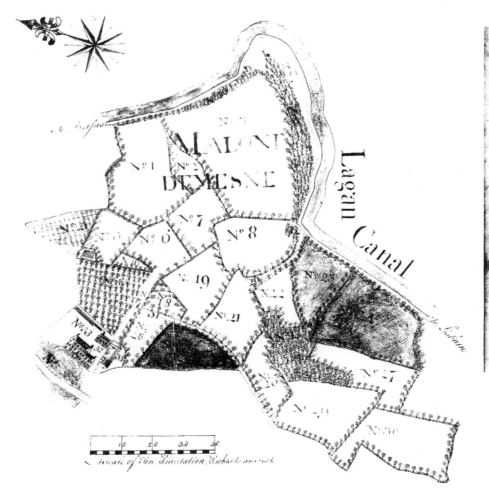

Map of Malone Demesne (below) with field names c. 1780 and a simplified copy (above).
The orientation of the north arrow on the original was incorrect.

The largest estate woodlands formed during this period may have been at Holywood House and Cultra House in north County Down. They were planted on the higher ground above both of the mansion houses and were first described in 1819, when they were well established. That above Holywood House (which stood in what is now the Palace Barracks) was said to have comprised mainly fir and beech laid out in straight lines and covering over 100 acres, the wood at Cultra about half this area but more picturesque.[58]

Maps provide a good source of information about the distribution of trees and woods around Belfast during this period, though the precision with which trees and other features were represented is of course open to question. Taylor and Skinner's *Maps of the roads of Ireland* surveyed in 1777 were, however, designed to be accurate enough to assist travellers by showing features that they would notice from the coach, such as churches, houses (roofed or ruined), windmills, hills, mounds, bogs and also trees and woodland.[59] The road maps for the Belfast area show trees at many of the big houses, including the properties near the shore north of Belfast called Jennymount, Grove and Fort William which seem to have been set in a fairly continuous belt of greenery. To the east of Belfast, trees are marked at big houses including those called Orangefield, Belmount, Castlehill, Thornyhill and Tullycarnet, while larger groups of trees are indicated around Belvoir and Purdysburn, south of Belfast. Lines of trees, probably grown along hedges, are shown by some roads, in particular the road to Antrim that passed through the gap between Cavehill and Carnmoney Hill, and along the Mall, a route from the south of Belfast to Cromac that was a popular walk for the well-to-do. Trees are not shown as being common in the Malone area, justifying its local name of 'the Plains'. Trees are also only occasionally shown on upland regions around Belfast (Castlereagh and Belfast Hills) though there are likely to have been at least some patches of scrub on the steep hill slopes around Belfast. This suggestion is supported by a notice placed by William Legg and John Ogle in 1777 concerning damage done to trees including the 'Upper and Underwood in the great Glynns of Collin', most likely a reference to woodland in Colin Glen.[60]

An additional source of information about woods is provided by notices of sales of timber in early issues of the Belfast News-Letter (Appendix 2). It is likely that only a very small proportion of the trees that were felled would have been advertised for sale, though these notices do help to identify the location and composition of woods. Most advertisements were placed by the big estates and the majority were for large pieces of timber, suggesting the presence of mature woods with tall trees. It is thought that many woods in Ireland were regularly cut (coppiced) at this time, though the only evidence of this practice from these Belfast advertisements is the sale of two ozier (osier willow) gardens at Stranmillis. Willows were grown in damp hollows known as gardens and the young pliable shoots cut every few years to use in trades such as basket making and by coopers to make hoops to bind together the staves of barrels.[61]

Letter from Charles Echlin, Bangor, to
Michael Ward, Dublin, 30th January, 1724.

I have got certain proof that John Wilson commonly called Whinny Wilson's son a Boy about 17 years old cut a small siccamore tree in the Plantation Park; there are three Ash Poles cut in the same place & it is very probable that he cut them, I gave a warrant to search but could not find them be pleased to send me orders how he shall be punished.

Letter from Charles Echlin, Bangor,
to Michael Ward, Dublin, 13th February,1724.

according to your orders I have examined the evidence about Wilson's son, which was that Bowman John Cowdan's servt found the Boy in ye Plantation cutting ye branches of the stick after it had been cut down. I have given a warrant to ye Constable to whipp him through the Town & have ordered the Father to give up his Land at alsaints next.[62]

Land owners were very protective of their trees though, even by the standards of the day, the punishment in this instance seems extreme.

Trees on the farm

For farmers in Ireland, preventing hard-won farmland from reverting to woodland or to bog was probably more of a priority than planting or protecting trees. This is borne out by an account of County Down from 1740, which noted that 'Soil runs into Wood, unless constantly kept open, and plowed, and the low Grounds soon degenerate into Moss or Bog where the Drains are neglected'.[63] Although there was little interest in protecting or planting trees on farms, farmers did have to plant hedges and, as the century progressed, it became common for leases to detail how hedges were to be constructed. For example, a standard printed lease for Donegall Estate lands of around 1742 informed tenants that they had to 'ditch the premises' and plant hedges of furrs (furze, a local name for gorse) or hawthorn with oak, ash, elm or beech trees and maintain the trees for ten years or pay a fine of £10.[64] A later printed lease for the Donegall Estate of around 1770 stated that land had to be divided by a 'good single Earth Ditch in straight Lines, with a Grip or Trench on one Side, six Feet wide at the Top, two Feet wide at the Bottom, and five Feet deep below the Surface of the Ground, and plant or sow the same with White-thorn or Crab-tree Quicks, or Furz'. The tenant also had to plant and preserve trees of oak, ash and elm every 20 feet.[65]

Reports of damage to hedges were common. This sometimes seems to have been caused by people frustrated by the way that hedges were increasingly defining land ownership and restricting access to the countryside. For example, a notice of 1755 complained of 'malicious and evil disposed persons' who had destroyed a new ditch and hedge between two farms in the townland of Edenderry. The farmer who had planted the hedge went so far as to state that he suspected his neighbour of doing the deed. On another occasion a farmer in Collinward, Carnmoney, publicly complained that a number of young ash planted in the hedgerow on the high road had been 'feloniously, most wickedly and maliciously broke down and destroyed'.[66]

Many early references to enclosures in the Belfast region referred to the use of gorse or crab apple (often called simply 'crab') for hedging. Perhaps these species would have made a stock-proof hedge when planted along the early type of boundary, which had a wide bank and deep trench. However, by the end of the 18th century, these field enclosures were being removed and remade with narrow banks that occupied much less space but would have required hedges that were more stock-proof.[67] This probably led to hawthorn becoming the preferred hedging species, because of its abundance of sharp thorns and the way that cut branches develop into a dense, interlocking network of twigs. No references from this period have been found to hedge laying, a form of management in which stems are cut half way through, bent over and woven into the hedge to form a more impenetrable barrier. However a notice placed by Thomas Boyd, Saddler, of High Street, Belfast in 1761 offered a solution to the difficult task of cutting prickly bushes with his 'Hedging Gloves for those who work among Thorns or Furz'.[68]

Town parks

Near Belfast there was a different kind of farming landscape in the 18th century, land described in maps and leases as 'town parks'. Today this designation is not in use, though a legal explanation can be found in 19th century court judgements. Town parks were lands close to a town or city, for the use of someone living in these urban areas that had higher value as 'accommodation land' than ordinary land let for farming purposes. Accommodation land was further defined as 'land held by a townsman for the supply, convenience and accommodation of his residence.' In addition, it was noted that town park holdings were generally small in size and that ordinary agricultural farms could not be considered as town parks.[69]

The way that town parks were used at this time can be deduced from old newspaper advertisements which sometimes referred to the letting of land in 'small parcels' and stressed the quality of the land, its accessibility to roads and bridges and proximity to Belfast.[70] A later comment about town parks in the Belfast News-Letter stated that they were 'allotments of ground in the vicinity of towns....chiefly fitted for the production of green and garden crops' and were close both to markets and to sources of abundant manure.[71]

One of Taylor & Skinner's Maps of the Roads of Ireland of 1777 that shows the Belfast area. Contrary to modern convention, the north arrow on these maps points to the lower left.

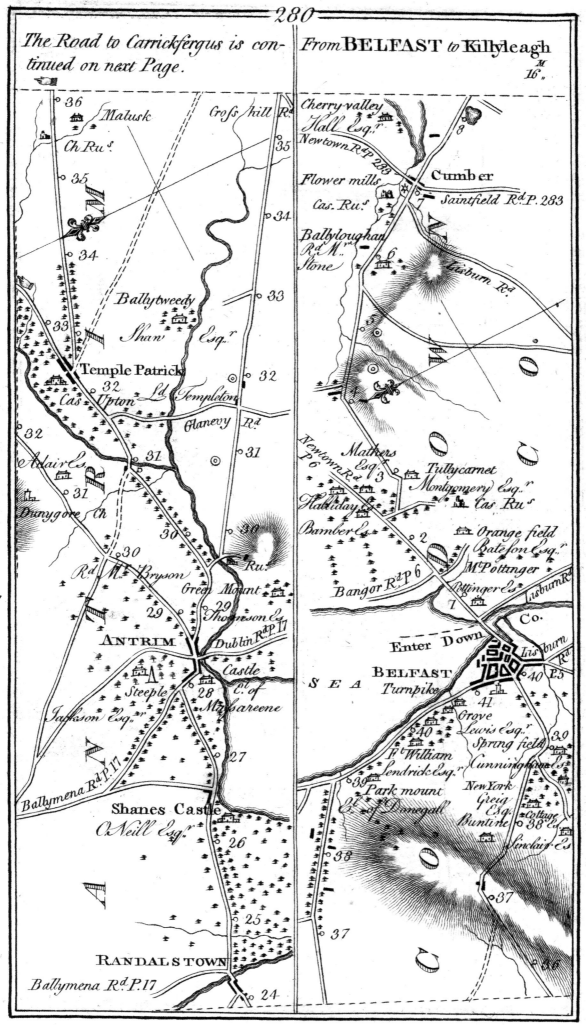

The Road to Carrickfergus is continued on next Page.

From **BELFAST** to Killyleagh
M
16"

Cherry valley
Hall Esq.r
Newtown Rd p. 283
Cumber
7
Flower mills
Saintfield Rd P. 283
Cas. Rus
Ballyloughan
Rd Mrs
Stone
6
Lisburn Rd

36
Mallusk
Crosshill Rd
35
Ch Rus
34
35
34
Ballytweedy
33
Shan Esq.r
Temple Patrick
32
Cas. Upton
Ld Templeton
Clanevy Rd
32
Adairs
31
31
Mathers Esq.r
Newtown Rd P 6
3
Tullycarnet
Montgomery Esq.r
Cas. Rus
Dunygore Ch
Halliday Es
Bamber Es
Orange field
Bateson Esq.r
Mr Pottinger
Rd Mr Bryson
30
Ru.
Bangor Rd P 6
2
Pottinger Es
Lisburn Rd
Green Mount
29
Co.
29
Thomson Es
Enter Down
Lisburn
ANTRIM
Dublin Rd p. 17
40 E 5
Castle
BELFAST
Steeple
28
El. of Massareene
SEA
Turnpike
Jackson Esq.r
41
27
Grove
Lewis Esq.r
Spring field
39
Ballymena Rd P. 17
40
F William
Lendrick Esq.r
Cunningham Es
39
New York
Greig
Esq.r
Shanes Castle
26
Park mount
O.Neill Esq.r
El. of Donegall
Cottage
Buntine
38 Es
Sinclair Es
38
25
37
RANDALSTOWN
37
Ballymena Rd P. 17
24

Terry Sculp

A CATALOGUE

OF

SEEDS, FRUIT-TREES, &c.

SOLD   BY

JOHN      BULLEN,

ENGLISH   SEED SHOP,

HIGH-STREET,   BELFAST.

1792.

SEEDS of ESCULENT ROOTS and PLANTS.

Asparagus Seeds
  Reading
  Gravesend
  Plants
Artichoke Plants
Broccoli
  early white
  late ditto
  early purple
  late ditto, or close-headed
  late dwarf do.
  brown Italian
  green
  Siberian
  sea green
Burnet
Brussel's sprouts
Beet
  red
  white
  green
Cauliflower
  early
  late
Cabbage
  early dwarf
  early Yorkshire
  early Russia
  early sugarloaf
  early Battersea
  early heart-shaped
  large Battersea
  large sugarloaf
  large winter
  Scotch, or cattle
  American
  red Dutch
  turnep-headed
  turnep-rooted
  Anjou
Carrot
  early horn
  long orange, or Sandwich
  early Russia
  early sugarloaf
  early Battersea
  early heart-shaped
  large Battersea
  large sugarloaf
  large winter
  Scotch, or cattle
  American
  red Dutch
  turnep-headed
  turnep-rooted
  Anjou
Carrot
  early horn
  long orange, or Sandwich
Colewort
  hardy green
Chou de Milan
Cardoons
Eschalot
Garlic
Kale
  green curled
  red ditto
  striped ditto
  sea
Leek
Onion
  James's, or long-keeping
  white Spanish
  brown Spanish
  Portugal
  silver-skinned for pickling
  Deptford
  Strasburgh
  blood-red
  Welsh
Parsnep
Radish
  early frame purple
  early short top
  early salmon
  white turnep
  purple turnep
  black Spanish
  white ditto
  salading
Rocambole
Skirrett
Savoy
  green curled
  dwarf
  yellow curled
Scorzonera
Salsify
Turnep
  early Dutch
  early stone
  white round
  green round
  red round
  Norfolk
  yellow
  French
Tarragon plants

SALLAD SEEDS.

Chervil
Cucumber
  early cluster
  early frame
  long prickly
  short prickly
  white Turkey

---

green Turkey
white Dutch
long green Roman
Celery
  new, or large piped
  solid stalked
  Italian upright
  large-rooted, or celeriac
Cress
  garden
  curled leaved
  water
  Belleisle, or broad leaved
Corn sallad
Endive
  green curled
  white ditto
  Batavian
Finochio
  Genoa forts
Lettuce
  white cos
  hardy green cos
  green cos
  Aleppo, or spotted do.
  forcing, or dwarf do.
  brown ditto
  black ditto
  Egyptian ditto
  imperial
  grand admirable
  capuchin
  brown Dutch
  royal brown Dutch
  tennis ball
  cabbage
  forcing cabbage
  hardy green
  Cilicia
  Prussian
  honey
  Dutch sugar
Love-style
Mustard
  white
  grand admirable
  capuchin
  brown Dutch
  royal brown Dutch
  tennis ball
  cabbage
  forcing cabbage
  hardy green
  Cilicia
  Prussian
  honey
  Dutch sugar
Love-style
Mustard
  white
  brown
Melon
  rock cantaleupe
  cantaleupe
  Romana and various others
Nasturtium
  tall
  dwarf
Purslane
  yellow
  green
Pompion
Radish salading
Rape
Spinach
  prickly
  French
Sorrel
  broad leaved
  French

LEGUMES.

Beans
  early mazagan
Lisbon
  long podded
  mazagan Windsor ditto
  broad Spanish
  toker
  Windsor
  Sandwich
  green Genoa
  dwarf fan
  white blossomed
  red blossomed
Beans kidney or French
  early yellow dwarf
  early white ditto
  early negro ditto
  late white ditto
  Canterbury ditto
  black speckled ditto
  large purple speckled ditto
  Battersea ditto
  we dutch ditto
  large white Dutch runners
  scarlet flowering ditto
  white flowering ditto
Peas
  es forcing
  ea Paddington
  ea golden hotspur
  Charlton
  Oned ditto
  Efreadings
  pea ditto
  transparent ditto
  tall rouncival
  dwarf do.
  Spa dwarf ditto

---

green ditto
Spanish morotto
pearl
egg
American
white rouncival
grey ditto
nonpareil
blue union
rose or crown
tall sugar
dwarf sugar
Ledman's dwarf
white split
green split
white boiling

SWEET and POT-HERBS.

Basil sweet
Balm
Borage
Clary
Fennel
Hyssop
Marjoram
  pot
  knotted or sweet
Marygold double
Parsley
  plain
  curled
  Hamburgh or large rooted
Savory
  summer
  winter
Thyme

ANNUAL FLOWERS.

*Those marked thus * require a gentle heat to raise them.*

Amaranthus
  tall red coxcomb *
  dwarf ditto *
  plain
  curled
  Hamburgh or large rooted
Savory
  summer
  winter
Thyme

ANNUAL FLOWERS.

*Those marked thus * require a gentle heat to raise them.*

Amaranthus
  tall red coxcomb *
  dwarf ditto *
  pyramidical red do *
  yellow ditto *
  tricolor *
  bicolor *
  purple globe *
  white ditto *
  striped ditto *
  love lies a bleeding
  princes feather
  tree
Alyssum sweet
  tall
  dwarf
Alkekengi
  blue
Aster China, superb, or French
  double white *
  ditto blue *
  ditto red *
  ditto flesh colour *
Aster China
  double purple *
  ditto white *
  ditto red *
  ditto purple striped *
  ditto red striped *
  ditto bonnet *
  ditto quilled *
  Italian double, various colours *
Browallia
Belvidere, or summer cypress
Basil bush
Balm Moldavian
Capsicum of sorts
Calendula
  Capensis
  Hybrida
Convulvulus major
  blue
  white
  scarlet
  minor blue
  ditto striped
Cucumber spurting
Caterpillar trefoil
Candy tuft
  large white
  small ditto
  large white rocket
  purple
  Crimson, or Normandy
Carthamus, or safflower
Cerinthe, or honey-wort
Cyanus variegated
Cannacorus
  yellow flowering
  red ditto
  spotted ditto, or Chinese
Diamond Ficoides, or Ice Plant

Clary
  red topped
  purple ditto
Cryfanthemum
  double yellow *
  double white *
  double quilled *
Catchfly Lobel's
  white
  red
Egg Plant
  purple *
  white *
  striped *
Flos adonis
Hedge-hog trefoil
Horn ditto
Hawkweed
  purple
  yellow
Hearts ease
Humble plant *
Jacobæa purple
Indian corn
  red
  yellow *
Kennia bladder
Lupine
  straw coloured
  yellow
  rose, or painted Lady
  large blue
  Dutch blue
  small blue
  white
  scarlet, or Tangier pea
Love apple
Lavatera
  white
Larkspur
  double tall rocket
  ditto dwarf rocket
  do. Neapolitan dwarf rocket
  ditto rose
rose, or painted Lady
  large blue
  Dutch blue
  small blue
  white
  scarlet, or Tangier pea
Love apple
Lavatera
  white
Larkspur
  double tall rocket
  ditto dwarf rocket
  do. Neapolitan dwarf rocket
  ditto rose
  ditto variegated
  branching
Lychnis mountain
Linaria Spanish
Marygold African
  orange coloured *
  lemon do. *
  quilled orange ditto *
  quilled lemon ditto *
  tall French *
  dwarf ditto
  sweet scented ditto
Marvel Peru
  white
  yellow
  striped
  sweet scented
Mignonette
  sweet scented
  upright ditto
  yellow ditto
Mallow
  oriental
  curled leaf
  tree ditto
Marygold yellow
Nettle Roman
Nolana prostrata
Nigella
  blue
  Spanish
Nasturtium
  tall
  white
  dwarf
Noli me tangere
Peas
  scarlet sweet scented
  purple ditto
  white ditto
  painted lady do.
  black ditto
  lord Anson blue
  winged
  Tangier, or scarlet lupine
  painted lady brown
  Grecian
  painted lady Spanish
  yellow
Palma Christi
  tall
  dwarf
Persicaria
  tall
  dwarf
Poppy
  double carnation
  double dwarf
Pink
  Indian, or China *
  Imperial China *
  Sweet William
Stock ten week
  French fcarlet

---

  scarlet
  purple
  white French
  white
  flesh-coloured
Scabious Globe
Sultan, sweet
  purple *
  white *
  yellow *
Strawberry spinach
Stramonium
  double white *
  double purple *
Sensitive plant *
Sunflower
  double tall
  double dwarf
Stock, Virginian
Snail trefoil
Tobacco
  Virginian, long leav'd
  round leav'd
Venus's looking-glass
  white
  blue
Venus's navelwort
Wallflower Prussian
  purple
  white
  scarlet
Xeranthemum
  purple
  white
Zinnia
  red *
  yellow *

BIENNIAL and PEREN- NIAL FLOWERS.

Auricula
  Agrimony, sweet-scented
  Alpine adonis
  Bee larkspur
  Siberian
  American
Xeranthemum
  purple
  white
Zinnia
  red *
  yellow *

BIENNIAL and PEREN- NIAL FLOWERS.

Auricula
  Agrimony, sweet-scented
  Alpine adonis
  Bee larkspur
  Siberian
  American
Balm of Gilead
Canterbury bell
Carnation
Columbine, double
  feathered
Campion, Rose
  red
  painted lady
Colutea, Ethiopian
Foxglove
  white
  red
  iron coloured
Flax, Siberian
Fraxinella
  white
  red
Goats rue
Globe thistle
Hollyhock
  double, various colours
  Chinese dwarf ditto
Honeysuckle, French
  white
  red
Honesty
  white
  purple
Lychnis
  scarlet
  white
Monkshood, Pyrenean
Polyanthus
Pink
  pheasant eye
  feathered
Primrose tree
Peas, everlasting
Reseda, or upright mignonette
Rocket, sweet
Stock July flower
  scarlet Brompton
  white ditto
  queen
  Twickenham purple
Stock
  white Dutch
Scabious sweet
Valerian
  Greek
  garden
Wallflower
  bloody
  yellow
  white

SEEDS to improve LAND.

Buck-wheat
Burnet

Broom, English
Canary
Clover
  white Dutch
  red
  hop, or trefoil
Colefeed, or rape
Flax
  English
  Riga
Furze
Grass
  Rye
  timothy
  bird
  cow's
  rib, or plantain
Hemp
  English
  Russian
Lucerne
Lentils
Maw-feed
Millet
Saintfoin
Tares
  spring
  winter
  white
Trefoil, or hop clover

FRUIT TREES

Proved to be true to their Kinds.

APPLES, 6d. h. each.

Golden pippin
Holland ditto
Newtown ditto
Kirton ditto
Embroidered do.
Ribstone ditto
Spencer's ditto
Lemon ditto
Aromatic ditto

FRUIT TREES

Proved to be true to their Kinds.

APPLES, 6d. h. each.

Golden Pippin
Holland ditto
Newtown ditto
Kirton ditto
Embroidered do.
Ribstone ditto
Spencer's ditto
Lemon ditto
Aromatic ditto
Monstrous ditto
Kentish ditto
Stone ditto
Whitmore's ditto
Ben Taylor's do.
Royal Ruffet
Pile's ditto
Aromatic ditto
Summer ditto
Loan's ditto
Nonfuch
Nonpareil
Permain
Scarlet ditto
Royal ditto
Summer ditto
Herefordshire do.
Syke house
Royal corpendu
French ditto
Golden Rennet
Carpenter ditto
Kitchen ditto
Norfolk Beefing
Transparent
Lincolnshire Holland
Winter July flower
Margreting
Dutch Codling
English ditto
Nonpareil ditto
Quince Apple
Cat's head
Norfolk Paradise
Margill
Kentish Fill-basket
American
Stubbard
Red Streak

APRICOTS, 1s. 8d. each.

Roman
Orange
Breda
Bruffelle
Moor Park, very fine
Algiers

CHERRIES, 1s. each.

Early May Duke
May Duke
Portugal ditto
Late arch ditto
Arch ditto
White Heart
Black ditto
Harrison's ditto
Bleeding ditto
Red ditto
Spanish black do.
Swedish ditto

Ox ditto
Morello
Croffian
Koroon
Striped fruited
Lackires
Lukeward
Mazard
Kentish
Double flowering

DUTCH CURRANTS, 2d. each.

FINE LANCASHIRE GOOSEBERRIES, 3d. each.

NECTARINES, 1s. 8d. each.

Elruge
  Red Roman
  Newington
  Early Pavie
  Duke de Tillie, new fort
  Brugnon

PEACHES, 1s. 2d.

Smith's Newington
  Early Ann
  Red Magdalen
  Montaubon
  Noblesse
  Admirable Pavie
  Royal George
  Scarlet Admirable
  Galland
  Grimwood's Royal George
  French Mignon

PEARS, 1s. 1d. each.

Jargonelle

Smith's Newington
  Early Ann
  Red Magdalen
  Montaubon
  Noblesse
  Admirable Pavie
  Royal George
  Scarlet Admirable
  Galland
  Grimwood's Royal George
  French Mignon

PEARS, 1s. 1d. each.

Jargonelle
Windsor
Brown Bugee
Orange Bergamot
Summer ditto
Autumn ditto
Easter ditto
Swiss ditto
Monsieur Jean
Crefan
Colmear
Vregoleufe
St. Germain
Chaumontelle
Cardiliac, or pound
Uvendale's St. Germain
Black Pear of Worcester
True Tarling
Pear de Auch
Auchin
Swan's Egg
Ganfeld's Burgundy
French Cuissmadame
Winter Ruffet
Hawkin's Bergamot
Lemon ditto

PLUMS, 1s. 1d. each.

Green Gage
  Blue ditto
Orleans
Red Bonum Magnum
Sermiona
Blue Imperatrice
Roche Corboon
Violet Damascene
Drop de or, or Cloth of Gold
Precose de Tours
Morocco
Reine Claude
Maitre ditto
Fotheringham

FRENCH ROSES.

	£	s	d
La Rose Unique Blanche de Provence		3	3
Moss Rose 1s. 1d. each, or £3 5 0 per hundred			
Rose de Meaux			
Dwarf Burgundy		1	1
Grand Sultana		1	1
Double Burnette Leaved	0	0	6
Wright's Province	0	0	6
Double Sweet briar	0	0	7
True Province	0	0	7

FINE GOLDEN RASPBERRIES, 2d. each.

SIBERIAN CRABS, 1s. 7d. each.

Flower Roots;—Russia Mattis,—also, Fine Early Forcing Potatoes 6d. per pound.

D. BLOW, PRINTER, HIGH-STREET, BELFAST.

DUBLIN SOCIETY,
&c.,&c.

Printed by W.^m; Sleater Dame street.
Printer to the Dublin Society;
And Sold by Allen & West,
N.º 15, Paternoster Row, LONDON.
MDCCXCIV.

4. The first great tree planting project

The first evidence we have of commercial plantations is from the early 18th century. Examples include a 'wood or nursery of ash' planted around 1706 at Moira that covered about an acre and a 'wood-farm' at Derryboy in County Down where 60 acres were planted with oak in 1732.[1] These trees were most likely grown because the clearance of more accessible woods was making timber scarce.[2] Government also recognised the need to increase planting as early as 1698 when the first of a series of acts were passed to encourage tenants to plant and care for trees. By the mid 18th century a number of organisations keen to promote agriculture were providing awards for tree planting and offering support for setting up local tree nurseries. By the second half of the 18th century the rate of tree planting started to gather momentum throughout Ireland and reached a peak around the period 1790 to 1840. For tenants and landowners alike, trees became recognised as a resource that would, in time, provide them with timber and also enhance the land.

Acts to encourage tree planting

The earliest acts required tenants to plant trees and restrict practices that would result in the damage or loss of trees. Subsequent acts gave tenants the incentive of an entitlement to a percentage of the trees at the end of the lease. By the second half of the 18th century, acts decreed that at the expiry of the lease the tenant could claim the trees or their value provided the trees had been registered. To establish the rights of the tenant to the trees, details of the plantings were given in sworn statements that were copied into ledgers and published in the Dublin Gazette. These tree lists now provide valuable information about the locations, species and numbers of trees planted by tenants and the date of registration.[3]

An advertisement of 1766 for the lease of Lambeg House near Dunmurry provides an early example of the rights of the person planting the trees being acknowledged. The notice stated that some trees had already been planted but that more were available in a nursery, and at the end of the lease an allowance would be made for trees planted by the tenant or the rights to the trees would be conveyed to the tenant.[4] However, it was only towards the end of the 18th century that large numbers of tenants started to register trees in Ireland. Throughout much of Ireland there was a trend for the number of registrations to increase into the early part of the 19th century, followed by a decline after the mid 1830s.[5] There does not seem to be a single explanation for the decline, though it is perhaps significant that in the Belfast region, which was relatively prosperous and did not suffer the full effects of the famine, quite large numbers of trees continued to be planted by tenants into the 1860s (see Appendix 3).

John Bullen's catalogue of 1792 is the earliest known to have survived for a Belfast nursery.
As well as a seed shop, John Bullen had a nursery in south Belfast, on land that was to become the Botanic Garden.

Plate 1.

P.46.

Fig.1.

Fig.II.

Fig.III.

Those interested in tree planting could get advice from books such as 'Practical Treatise on Trees' by Samuel Hayes (1794),
which contains this wonderful illustration of a tree transplanting machine.

Premiums for planting

The Dublin Society (today the Royal Dublin Society) played a significant role in developing interest in tree planting. Premiums (awards) and medals were given for specified tree planting projects, for tree nurseries and for planting willows and poplars for uses like basket weaving. Through its awards schemes the Society also stressed the need for fencing new woods to keep cattle from eating saplings. The premium system was introduced in 1739, initially funded by members of the Society, though later by the Irish Parliament.[7]

Some landowners near Belfast supported the early Dublin Society schemes, most notably Arthur Hill (Viscount Dungannon) of Belvoir Park, who received two gold medals for tree planting in the year 1766. One medal was for planting the greatest number of Weymouth pine in Ulster (717 trees), the other for planting the greatest number of oaks in Ulster (7,180 trees).[8] The oaks were recorded as having been planted at Belvoir, and it is tempting to suggest Arthur Hill may have collected the acorns used for this scheme from the oak trees then growing at this site.

In northeast Ireland, the role developed by the Dublin Society was soon eclipsed by local farming societies that promoted agriculture and tree planting. The first agricultural organisation to be set up in the region was the Farmers Society of the four Lower Baronies of the County of Antrim, founded in 1755 as a non-political club to promote husbandry and industry. It stated that it was emulating the example of the Dublin Society and promoted planting, including field hedges and osier (willow) beds. In the early advertisements it was stated that the hedges had to be planted with hawthorn quicks, though later crab apple and wildings (wild trees) were also allowed, and there was a requirement to include spaced timber trees. In 1756 the Down Society for the Encouragement of Agriculture and other useful Arts was founded, and advertised prizes of up to £10 for planting hedges and orchards and for creating nurseries. There were other awards, including one for the person who 'produces at Downpatrick the best Barrel of mild ale Brewed with Barley Malt the growth of the County of Down' (there were also awards for the second, third, fourth and fifth best barrels of ale). Elsewhere in the region hedge and tree planting was encouraged by the Ballymoney Club, the Farming Society for Carrickfergus and Kilroot Parishes and the Lower Massereene and Glenavy Farming Society.[9]

The farming societies were to some degree self-serving organisations. For example the Ballymoney Club specifically stated that the distribution of premiums would be confined to the tenants of the subscribers. In effect, this meant that landlords were giving back some of the income they received from tenants to support the improvement of estate lands. However, these schemes were undoubtedly of value in popularising the planting of trees, hedgerows and orchards.

The Dublin Society discontinued its awards for tree planting in 1808, apparently because there had been fraudulent claims. The farming societies in the northeast of Ireland also moved away from promoting tree planting around this time. However, nothing has been found to suggest that this was because of problems with the schemes. Rather it seems that interest in planting by farmers was waning and the societies were becoming drawn towards encouraging farm production and organising activities with a more social aspect such as agricultural shows and ploughing matches.

The Brocioli seed I sent you by Post and hope it has gone safe; I cant find out what you mean by field Lupins, it is not known in the general seed shops about St. James's nor in Wises Garden but I will enquire at the Italian Gardeners you mention and if I find it send it by Post. There is no such thing as the seed or Cones of the Cedar of Lebanon to be had, the Tree you mentioned in the Phisick Gardens at Chelsey, did last year for the first time bear one Single Cone, so you may be sure none of the seed contain'd in it is to be procur'd by me. There was not one seed of the Beechmast saved last year, the violent Rains destroy'd them all; the Want of these can be no great disappointment to you for you may be served with any number of the Plants you please, from English or Irish seed, at an easie price by two Gardeners in the County of Tyrone. You observe two alterations in the names of the Trees from the catalogue you sent me, how it happened I can't tell; the change was made after I left the Garden. They may be different names for the same Trees or perhaps may doe as well.[6]

Prior to the advent of local nurseries, obtaining plants could be difficult. This extract of a letter that Michael Ward, a wealthy landowner in County Down, received in 1725/6 gave what must have been frustrating news from London about his planting plans.

Development of nurseries

Traditionally, trees were imported, were grown by landowners for their own use or were obtained from a cottage industry of local suppliers who occasionally advertised sales of trees.[10] The setting up of local nurseries made trees much more available. The development of this industry in the northeast of Ireland can be traced through newspaper advertisements which often contained details of the trees that were available and the names of the nursery owner, some of whom were former gardeners to the gentry.

The first advertisement noted for a nursery dates from 1749, when Samuel Pue of Armagh had for sale trees, quicks and a range of fruit trees, including grafted dwarf apple trees said to be suitable for kitchen gardens. In the following year James Sloan, described as a gardener and nurseryman at Edenderry, between Belfast and Lisburn, had forest trees from 3 to 12 feet high, though later in 1758 he was selling his stock (oak, elm, beech, ash, sycamore, lime, chestnut and hornbeam) as the land was to be used for other purposes. William Dick in County Armagh advertised the sale of apple trees in 1755 and offered to plant the trees and replace any that died in the first year. Around this time George Cutler also had a nursery in County Armagh.[11]

During the 1760s a dispersed pattern of nurseries developed throughout northeast Ireland. These included businesses at Holymount near Downpatrick, Armagh, Moira and at Sheanogstown, Antrim.[12] There were two nurseries in Lisburn, both run by people by the name of Johnson. One was William Johnson at 'the Orange-Tree', the other was Arthur Johnson of Bow Lane. Both were advertising the sale of asparagus in the early 1760s, and later in this decade both were selling fruit trees, forest trees, shrubs, thorn and crab quicks. In 1768 Arthur Johnson's nursery was taken over by his son (also called Arthur) and was still in business 14 years later, when he had large quantities of common and weeping birch and alder for sale. William Johnson advertised the sale of trees and also seeds until December 1797, when he sold his stock, 'being determined to quit that business'.[13]

Perhaps the best known early nursery near Belfast was started by William Bell, who was gardener at Belvoir Park and later gardener to Lord Viscount Dunluce and Lady Antrim. While in these jobs in 1774 and 1775 he was offering for sale garden and flower seeds, plant roots and various kinds of forest tree seed.[14] In 1776 he left his employment and became keeper of the Great Inn in Comber though he continued to sell garden and tree seed.[15] In the following years he expanded his business and in 1789 received a Dublin Society grant for a two-acre nursery.[16] He later went into partnership with David Hervey who in 1800 took over the Comber nursery, while William Bell opened a seed shop in Belfast. These businesses continued after the death of William Bell in 1805 and David Hervey in 1810, with William's wife taking over the seed shop and John Hervey running the Comber nursery (now called Nurseryville).[17] John Hervey started a new agricultural and garden seed business at the Bank Buildings

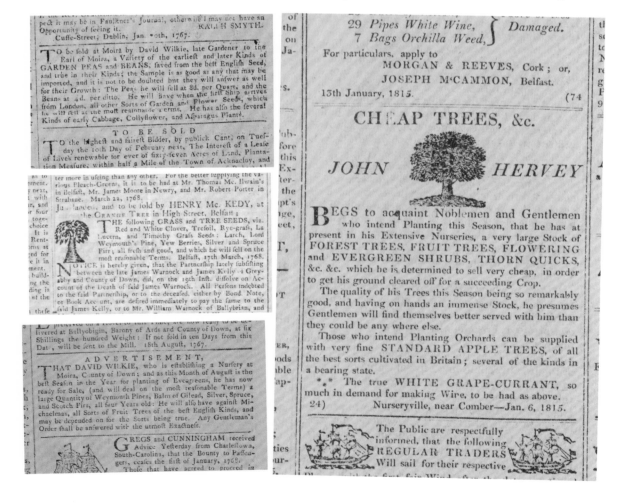

in Belfast and in the nursery concentrated on growing fruit trees, shrubs and exotic plants. He also specialised in Irish yew, of which he boasted he had 'more good plants of it than any other individual in the kingdom, and could send a parcel to London by the steamer any week.' However, tragedy was sadly to end this long-established family business. In 1829, when aged 43, John Hervey was bitten by a pet dog and developed hydrophobia (rabies). The local newspaper described in detail his final days and death, lucid to the end but unable to drink.[18]

A number of nurseries were developed from the 1770s onwards in the immediate vicinity of Belfast. Many were run by people who had a nursery in the suburbs (often in the grounds around their home) and a seed shop in town, and chief among these were businesses run by John Bullen, Daniel Robertson and Edward Lindsay.

John Bullen, proprietor of the 'English Seed Shop' (first in High Steet then Ann Street), was importing fruit trees together with roses and flower roots by 1791. In subsequent years he also sold thorn quicks and set up a nursery in south Belfast, at Friar's Bush. In 1799 John Bullen had at his nursery several thousand two-year-old thorn quicks, larch from two to six feet, four-year-old Scotch firs (Scots pine) and fruit trees. In 1804 his stock included many thousands of seedling beech trees. However, as the result of a law suit, the nursery closed.[19]

Daniel Robertson came to Belfast from London and initially set up a nursery at Turf Lodge, though in 1799 he advertised the sale of the entire stock of his nursery, which comprised fruit trees, several thousand forest trees, thorn quicks and 'a variety of curious plants'. By 1800 he had a house and nursery by the shore at Whitehouse and he also opened a seed shop in Belfast (in North Street then Castle Street). He later sold the house and had a nursery at Ballynafeigh, though on his death in 1810 the nursery had only a few thousand trees of the more common species.[20]

Edward Lindsay, who had a seed shop at Donegall Street, developed a nursery called Lillliput in the grounds of the house of this name near the lough shore north of Belfast. The earliest advertisements placed by Lindsay were in the 1790s, and in February 1800 his stock included 100,000 two and three-year-old thorn quicks. He also advertised rooms to let and promoted the virtues of tepid and cold sea baths that he had created at 'Lilliput nursery garden'. These ventures do not seem to have been successful and in 1802 all his nursery stock was auctioned. He retained his seed shop and was soon selling trees from a nursery called Roseville and then at Amyville, Malone. Lindsay became ingenious at encouraging sales. For example, in November 1814 he auctioned bundles of trees for planting around houses that he termed 'cottage parcels'. These parcels comprised 25 ornamental forest trees together with orchard species to provide fruit and nuts. Interestingly, the advertisement did not suggest that the forest trees should be planted for their timber value, but rather appealed to the landowner to enhance the appearance of their garden and to create a living legacy:

> 25 ORNAMENTAL FOREST TREES, Some large enough to furnish and shelter the FARMER'S MANSION and his COTTAGER'S HABITATION; and may be planted in groups, in Lawns, Hedge-Rows, Avenues etc; making the residence ornamental, and enhancing the value annually; so as to enliven the scene to the Traveller, making the Country look pleasant and cheerful, that Fathers or Heads of Families may hand down to Posterity, growing monuments of their remembrance, to their Children's Children.

During the early 19th century some nurseries grew into sizable businesses. For example, when Edward Lindsay's Belfast Nursery closed in 1834 it included a stock of 2 million seedling forest trees and several hundred thousand transplanted 3 to 5-year-old thorns.[21] Another Belfast nursery run by a Mr Farrell had a stock of 3 million thorn quicks for sale in 1840.[22] Outside the immediate area around Belfast, the growth of the Armagh nursery run by William Penton was remarkable. He developed a nursery that appears to have been started in the 1770s by Richard Penton, who had been gardener to the Earl of Clanbrassil and to the Lord Primate. By 1815 William Penton had a nursery covering nearly 20 acres that was stocked with half a million transplanted forest trees and one million one and two-year-old tree seedlings. There were also 8,000 apple trees and over 4 million thorn quicks, as well as shrubs and roses.[23]

Imports of trees

Some of the earliest nursery advertisements mention imports of trees, plants and seeds. For example, Samuel Pue of Armagh included in his advertisement of 1749 English, Dutch and French elms. Belfast merchant Henry McKedy regularly imported tree and grass seed from the 1760s, and merchants Campbell, Donnaldson and Co. imported 'French firr seed' in 1766 and 1767. David Wilkie, who had been gardener to the Earl of Moira, an estate famous for its exotic trees, had a nursery at Moira from 1767 to 1792 and in his in his advertisement of March 1769 offered hardy American tree seed and 'various Kinds of Pines, Firs, Spruces and Cedars, etc too tedious to be inserted here at large.' In the following decades, as interest in gardening and landscaping developed, an ever-increasing range of imported ornamental trees was advertised for sale in the newspapers from merchants, nurserymen or at auctions of trees at Belfast dock.[24]

In the 1770s and 1780s there were a number of advertisements in the Belfast News-Letter for hawthorn from Dublin. These trees were most likely brought north because demand for hawthorn for hedging around Belfast was exceeding the local supply. Evidence for this is also provided by the only advertisement noted in the Belfast News-Letter requesting tree seed, which was in October 1772 when thirteen pence a bushel was offered for 40-50 bushels of haws (hawthorn berries).[25]

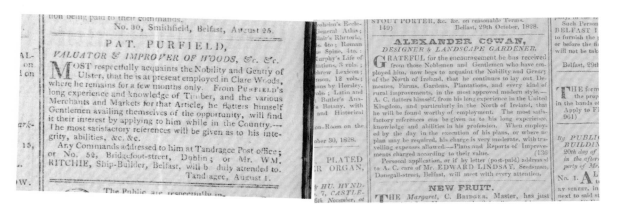

Planters and landscapers, woodland managers and valuers

Unfortunately, we have almost no information about the laying out of the big estates around Belfast, though we do know something of the local people involved in the landscaping profession. For example, in 1777 Kenneth Sutherland advertised in the Belfast News-Letter to lay out gardens, pleasure grounds, hothouses and vine houses. He was gardener to the Countess of Antrim and was almost certainly the person of this name who had been gardener at Belvoir Park. In the following decades other local men who became involved in landscaping included R. O'Donnell, who styled himself 'groundsworkman, planter and seedsman' and William Pink who had been planter to Earl O'Neill.[26]

One who toiled in the gardens of Malone and now rests in Friar's Bush graveyard.

By the end of the century woods planted in earlier decades would have required management. Those who saw a business opportunity in this work included Mr Dutton of 39 Paradise-row, Dublin, who advertised in the Belfast News-Letter in 1801 to undertake a range of agricultural work including thinning plantations. The first advertisements noted for woodland valuers also date from this period. These professionals travelled the country seeking employment as they went and included Dan O'Brien of Dublin who based himself in County Armagh and offered his services in valuing and selling timber on the fairest of terms and a gentleman called Pat Purfield who announced that he was visiting the north of Ireland seeking work as a 'valuator and improver of woods.'[27]

5. Views of Victorian Belfast

By the early 19th century, tree planting had started to make a noticeable difference to the landscape of the Belfast region, particularly on the well-drained, fertile soils found in much of the Lagan Valley and lands towards the shores of Belfast Lough. These areas provided ideal conditions for trees to flourish. Trees became a common feature around stately houses, farms and cottages. The writer George Benn noted in 1823 that the houses of even the poorest farmers in the lowlands around Belfast were 'protected or embellished, more or less, with the tall ash or the humble sallow'.[1] On the higher ground it was more difficult to establish trees, though before the end of the century many upland stream valleys and some hill slopes were planted.

The need for firewood and timber must have been an important reason for planting trees, though sale notices for villas in the early to mid 19th century often emphasised the attractive setting provided by new plantations. The importance placed on planting to enhance the landscape is also seen from tree lists registered by tenants. These were predominantly not single species plantations designed to maximise timber yield but mixed woodlands, often with a surprisingly wide range of broadleaved and coniferous trees together with species such as laurel and holly as an understorey. Sometimes decorative species such as laburnum, rowan and cherry were included, most likely for planting on the fringes of the woods and around the house.[2]

In the Belfast region beech was the dominant broadleaved tree in plantations registered during the earlier decades of the 19th century, though some new woods had large numbers of oak, ash, sycamore or elm. A few sites had quite large numbers of fast-growing smaller trees like birch and alder.[3] Throughout Ireland the percentage of conifers (in particular larch) in registered tree lists increased during the Victorian era.[4]

By the mid 19th century, a growing number of conifer species were being introduced and these were often planted as specimen trees, as reflected in an 1868 advertisement for the auction of conifers at Andrew Daly's nurseries in Newry. Here one could have bought trees including giant redwood, monkey puzzle, western red cedar, deodar cedar, Lawson cypress and Monterey pine at 4 to 10 feet in height 'all closely and well furnished, and handsome shape, and will give immediate effect when planted in Lawns or Carriage Drives etc.'[5] Some landowners became particularly enthusiastic planters of exotic conifers. One such was Mr Whitla of Dunedin, Cave Hill, who was reported in the 1850s to have planted specimens of all of the hardy coniferous trees that had as yet been introduced.[6] Exotic trees were also planted around smaller properties, most noticeably the monkey puzzle which, with its unusual shape and extraordinary foliage, became emblematic of the Victorian villa garden. The increased planting of evergreen trees and shrubs, including privet and other evergreen hedging, must have been particularly noticeable during winter months when their green foliage contrasted with the bare branches of most of the trees in native woodlands.

Detail of a map of County Down by James Williamson surveyed in 1810.
Tree planting in demesnes and the woods above Holywood House and Cultra are shown in great detail.

51

Macedon. *The beautiful FARM of MACEDON, containing 14A. 1R. 9P. Plantation Measure, on which has been lately built a handsome, fashionable, convenient and roomy Mansion, with suitable offices. The Land is in the highest condition, having been lately both limed and manured; there are 9000 of the most valuable and ornamental Trees and Shrubs planted last year, and all in fine health. The Garden has been made at a great expense, and now cropped full with all kinds of Vegetables. – The real beauty of the place is too well known to require any encomiums. (Sale notice, 26/10/1804)*

Pine-Hill, Drumbo. *The House is convenient and well furnished…The Garden and Orchard contain one Acre, planted with the best Fruit Trees. The Farm consists of thirty-three Acres, in good heart, and well inclosed, on which there is a thriving Plantation of Forest Trees of 35 years growth, besides Hedge Rows. The House is situated about five Miles from Belfast, and three from Lisburn, and enjoys the view of a Country which may vie with any in Ireland for beauty and improvement. (Sale notice, 3/1/1806)*

Throne. *The THRONE-HOUSE and FARM, situate at the base of the CAVE-HILL…The house is large and commodious, and having lately undergone a thorough repair, is fit for the reception of a respectable family…The Garden, which contains upwards of an Acre, is in excellent order, and well stocked with sound and productive Fruit Trees of the choicest description. The Farm contains 36 Statute Acres of prime Land in a high state of cultivation, well fenced and drained, with an abundance of Spring Water in each field in the driest season; the whole skirted and ornamented with forest trees of nearly 50 years' growth. The salubrity and beauty of the situation are so well known that any comment is unnecessary. (Sale notice, 23/8/1839)*

By the early 19th century sale notices for properties frequently highlighted the beautiful setting provided by plantations, ornamental trees and orchards. Extracts from the Belfast News-Letter.

The lowlands

By the early 19th century the good agricultural land of the Lagan Valley had become attractive, prosperous and well-wooded. Many writers were enthusiastic about the appearance of this gateway to Belfast, including Henry Bayly who in 1834 penned what was perhaps the most effusive praise:

> The various beauties of plantation and bleach-green, of lake and waterfall, of plain and mountain, of grove and woodland; - where sloping hills, magnificent vistas, verdant vales, fertile fields, high cultured grounds, and inviting villas shine, indicate to the traveller that he is in the Eden of Erin! It is almost impossible to bring any country to a state of higher perfection, or find a happier display of scenery than that surrounding Lisburn.[7]

Much of this landscape was formed from estate lands of well-managed farms and demesnes that typically included woods, plantations and parkland. Some of these estates had a long history of occupation by generations of a single family, and in these instances a gradual evolution of the landscape could be expected. However, many demesnes that were put up for sale and were therefore at risk of being divided up not only survived the Victorian era with their grounds intact, but were enhanced and developed by succeeding owners.

Malone was a typical example of an estate that was long associated with one family. Here William Legg undertook improvements including the planting of 6,350 trees, which he registered in 1799 (Appendix 3). Additional evidence of his tree planting is given by the recent dating of one tree in the row of spaced oaks along what is now the boundary between Barnett Park and the Queen's University pitches. This tree (and most likely the rest of the row) started to grow in 1810.[8] A description of the property from this period referred to his house, 'an edifice of most respectable aspect' and plantations that were separated from the road by an extensive lawn bounded by a low painted paling (fence).[9]

Improvements at Malone continued through the 19th century. An estate map of 1825 shows the demesne as a largely agricultural landscape of meadows with some orchards, though parkland was being created. There were lawns dotted with trees by the house, belts of trees planted along some hedge lines and new areas of woodland created along steeper ground paralleling the River Lagan. Around this time a new mansion house was built in the centre of the demesne, on a hill top where there were fine views over the grounds and surrounding countryside. By 1829 the Upper Malone Road had been diverted away from the demesne, an operation that doubtless enhanced views from the mansion but earned Mr Legg the

Veteran larch at Malone Demesne (Barnett Park) with a girth of 5.65m at 1.2m.

disapproval of his neighbours, who now had to travel by a more circuitous route.[10] In subsequent decades the grounds continued to be modified, with an opening up of the landscape to create extensive parkland with large, spreading trees (mainly oak and beech) and patches of woodland. The orchards and small agricultural fields were eventually removed, though some rows of tall-growing trees that had been planted along field boundaries were retained and can still be seen today.[11]

Another example of a demesne with a long continuity of management is Belvoir Park. In the beginning of the 19th century the demesne created by the Hill family was acquired by three businessmen who, not long afterwards, advertised to break it up and sell the land for farms, each of 20-50 acres. However this did not happen as, in 1811, Robert Bateson (formerly of Orangefield in east Belfast) acquired the mansion and much of the surrounding land. The Batesons were to own Belvoir throughout the 19th century and not only retained old parkland trees but also undertook additional planting in the demesne.[12]

The Wilmont Estate of upper Malone, created by the Stewart family, had a more chequered history. It was well landscaped by the 1830s, when it was described as having plantations of different ages, and an estate map of 1842 shows spaced parkland trees by the house, woodland along a bank paralleling the River Lagan and planting strips along some of the boundaries of the demesne.[13] However, in 1844 the estate was mortgaged to the Northern Banking Company and although the new owner Alexander McKenzie Shaw further enhanced the grounds by planting over 20,000 trees,[14] he in turn fell into debt and in 1854 a map was prepared indicating how the grounds could be divided up and sold in lots.[15] Wilmont was to change hands several more times, but the demesne remained intact and the presence today of many large trees with a circumference of 3m or greater (Appendix 4) is proof that the successive inhabitants of the big house were careful to retain the landscape.

At some properties large areas of new woodland and parkland were laid out during the 19th century. For example a recent tree survey of the grounds of Stranmillis (now Stranmillis University College) suggests that, with the exception of a few mainly non-native veteran trees that may date from the 18th century, most of the trees seen here today represent extensive early to mid 19th century plantings. This suggestion is supported by recent tree ring analysis of two large fallen trees, which have given start dates of around 1800 for a sweet chestnut and 1866 for an oak.[16] The tree survey also revealed that the trees planted at Stranmillis were an unusual species mix, being dominated by beech and sweet chestnut (Appendix 4).

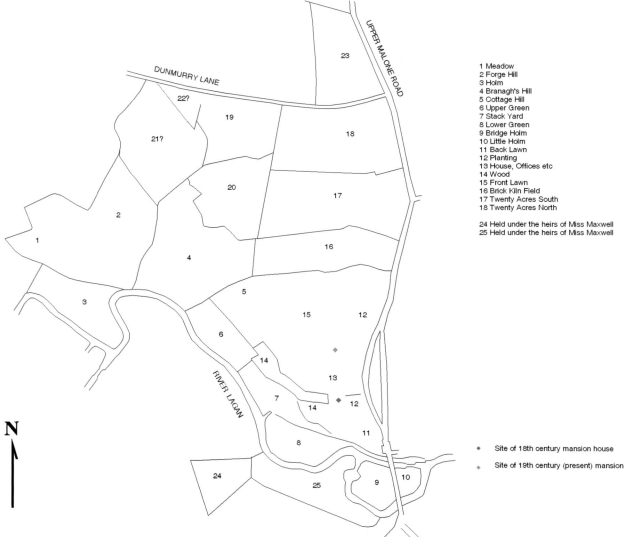

1 Meadow
2 Forge Hill
3 Holm
4 Branagh's Hill
5 Cottage Hill
6 Upper Green
7 Stack Yard
8 Lower Green
9 Bridge Holm
10 Little Holm
11 Back Lawn
12 Planting
13 House, Offices etc
14 Wood
15 Front Lawn
16 Brick Kiln Field
17 Twenty Acres South
18 Twenty Acres North

24 Held under the heirs of Miss Maxwell
25 Held under the heirs of Miss Maxwell

♦ Site of 18th century mansion house
♦ Site of 19th century (present) mansion

Illustration of the first house at Wilmont and surrounding planting from an estate map of 1842 with a simplified copy of the field boundaries with field names copied from this map.

A demesne that seems to have been largely the creation of the early 19th century was Ormeau in south Belfast. The Donegall family, who had been absentee landlords during much of the 18th century, returned to Belfast in 1802 and in 1807 moved from a town house to what was then countryside across the river at Ormeau. Here the second Marquis of Donegall developed a Tudor-style house with extensive grounds.[17] There were already some trees in the area,[18] though large-scale planting was undertaken in the laying out of the demesne. The landscaping, which was directed by the Marchioness of Donegall, was cryptically described in one tourist guide of 1830. This noted that 'the traveller will at once perceive, that in the laying out of the grounds and the arrangement of the plantations, it was no common mind which directed the hands employed.' Another commentator was less guarded, stating that 'the grounds are tame, the place narrow, the trees young, even the house is not suited to the family, tho' it has cost a great deal of money.'[19]

Aside from the big estates, there was tree planting by small landowners and tenants throughout the region, including sites surprisingly close to Belfast, such as at Cromac, the site of the former Cromac Wood. Here 1,100 trees (mainly larch, spruce and beech) were planted in 1801 by William Irvin, described in his lease of the land as a butcher.[20]

A property close to Belfast known as Cranmore (the location of the old sweet chestnut trees referred to in Chapter 2) became the site of an experimental garden. This was laid out by John Templeton, who had a keen interest in natural history, in particular botany. He started to cultivate flowers about 1786 and by 1793 was growing exotic plants, some of which he kept first in the hothouse and then greenhouse before planting out. He also encouraged the growth of plants by selecting the most appropriate soil and location.[21] John Templeton communicated with botanical gardens in Britain and Ireland, in particular the Dublin gardens run by Mr Underwood at Glasnevin and Mr Mackay at Trinity College, institutions that regularly sent him plant material. Other specimens came from nurseries, especially 'Harvey's nursery near Comber' (most likely the business run by Bell and Hervey), and from private gardens including on several occasions Lady Dufferin at Ballyleidy (Clandeboye).[22]

Cranmore comprised a long, narrow strip of land that extended from the sands of the Malone ridge down to the Blackstaff River at the Bog Meadows.[23] The best land would have been on the sandy soils of Malone, the area near the house, and it is probably here that John Templeton did his gardening. We can gain an impression of the area from notes he made in his diary, which include reference to the oak tree field, orchard field, highway field and spring field (the last named having a fairy thorn) and to an alder grove, larch grove and avenue. The avenue most likely extended from the Malone Road to the house, and would have incorporated the three old sweet chestnut that shaded the main façade of the property. At Cranmore there was in addition a kitchen garden, orchard (where there was a pond), raspberry bed and, on land held from a neighbour, Mr Wilson of Maryville, gooseberry bushes.[24] Unfortunately, we know little about John Templeton's experimental planting and the only description that has been found of the gardens is one all too brief note:

> Mr. Templeton, the celebrated botanist, resides within less than two miles of Belfast, and his garden will afford a rich treat to all who are engaged in botanical pursuits - they will find many rare plants thriving in their appropriate soils, and in an arrangement which nature seems particularly to dictate and to delight in - the ground is not dotted with direction sticks, which, though extremely useful, have a most sepulchral appearance, and give, as least to me, the garden of nature much the aspect of a grave-yard.[25]

John Templeton died in 1825. In his biography published four years later it was said that, excepting the sweet chestnut and some oaks, he had planted the trees then growing at Cranmore. In his diary we can find details of some of these trees, including the dwarf spruce, *Picea abies* 'Clanbrassiliana' which he was sent from Glasnevin Botanic Garden in 1808. It would have been a prized rarity though it may not have survived, as two years later he received a second specimen, this time from Tollymore, where Lord Clanbrassill had grown several (said to have been from a parent plant found at Moira). This was a feature of the gardens for many years though it grew imperceptibly. It was described in 1844 as being only three foot high with a stem just two inches in diameter.[26]

The Lagan Valley in the 19th century became a carefully-managed landscape where woodlands merged into grasslands and wetlands. It would be wrong to imagine the countryside around Victorian Belfast as in any way idyllic; factories were pouring polluting smoke into the atmosphere, river life was frequently damaged by discharges from flax ponds and around lower Ormeau the foul smell of the Blackstaff River gave rise to endless complaints over decades.[27] However, in the long-established woodlands of the Lagan Valley wildlife flourished. Ralph Tate, in his guide to the flora of the region published in 1863, listed the best sites around Belfast for woodland plants as Colin Glen, Malone, Newtownbreda and Belvoir.[28] Pine martens, creatures of woods, were recorded by the naturalist William Thompson in the grounds of Malone House and at Belvoir Park where he noted that a marten inflicted a severe bite on the hand of a boy who unexpectedly found it in a magpie's nest which he intended to rob! There are also references from this period to buzzards and a heronry at Belvoir and there is some evidence to suggest the rookery that today is a feature of these woods may have been present since the 18th century.[29]

In the north of County Down the best place to see trees in the 19th century seems to have been at Cultra, described in the 1850s in the florid prose of the local surgeon, Thomas Kelly,[30] and the more academic writings of J. Drummond.[31] Both of these authors were attracted by large trees with spreading branches that must have developed in a long-established open parkland landscape.

> Few situations can be more imposing or romantic than Cultra. In different parts it is overshadowed by numerous luxuriant oak trees of singularly beautiful form and growth. The gigantic size attained by some is surprising, and their long graceful branches reaching to the ground, produce an effect not unlike what we have heard related by some relatives, of the famed Banyan groves, in the plains of India. Several rare wild plants, important in botanical science, also decorate the demesne. (Kelly, 1850)

> There is nothing remarkable about this place that we could observe, except the undulating park with its fine trees. There is a plain kitchen garden, but neither it nor the mansion is in good repair.
> A large Huntingdon Willow tree, by the side of the approach near the house, measures 13 feet 6 inches in circumference between the swell of the roots and that of the branches. It branches into two limbs, each 6 feet in circumference. A Beech tree near to the Willow measures in circumference, at breast height, 14 feet, with a clean bole 20 feet in height. Another, 11 feet at same height, with a bole 30 feet in height; spread of branches, 50 feet diameter. We measured four Evergreen Oaks, which, for beauty of outline, health and freshness of foliage, could not be excelled. The circumference of bole, at about breast height, is 8 feet, and the spread of branches 50 feet diameter of one of these; of another, 8 feet, with 6 feet in height of a bole – spread of branches, 50 feet; the other two 5 feet circumference each – spread of branches, 44 feet diameter. A fine Spanish Chestnut measured 13 feet 4 inches in circumference, at breast height. These, with a few fine Horse Chestnut trees, grow near to the house. (J. Drummond, 1854)

Along the northern coastal strip of County Down large-scale planting started before the end of the 18th century. Rockport Farm was described in 1799 as having 'a Grove of full-grown Trees, to which has been added a small Shrubbery' and a farm called West Brook, located near the shore between Belfast and Holywood, had in 1809 over 15,000 forest trees of from 10 to 15 years age.[32] Planting continued in farms and in the grounds of large villas that were built along this coast during the 19th century. Woodlands were sometimes created on an impressive scale, such as at Ballyrobert, where Mr R. F. Gordon planted 13,838 trees in 1843 and 17,072 trees the following year (Appendix 3). The planting was typical of many such schemes with a mixture of conifers with oak, ash, beech and elm and small numbers of ornamental trees such as laburnum, scarlet thorn, maple, holly, yew and birch.

Some woodlands were created away from the coast on less favourable ground. One such attempt was by William Pirrie at Conlig, between Newtownards and Bangor. The ground was rocky, uneven and unsuitable for growing crops and in the 1820s the nurseryman John Hervey was employed to design the plantation, which was about 30 acres in extent and included larch, Scots pine, spruce, ash, oak, elm, beech and alder. Around 400 apple and other fruit trees were also planted on lower ground. Members of the Belfast Horticultural Society visited the site in 1831 and, after noting that the trees were thriving and that what they described as a wild waste was becoming an ornament, the Society presented the owner with a silver medal and hoped that other landowners would emulate his example.[33]

The most extensive woods in the region were created near Bangor at Ballyleidy, the Clandeboye Estate. This was largely the work of the first Marquis of Dufferin and Ava, who inherited the property in 1841. He developed the existing woodland in the demesne and also planted swathes of the adjacent estate grounds. The earliest record found to this project dates from 1843, when a contractor was sought to plant 30 acres with forest trees.[34] Major works included moving the Craigantlet-Bangor road, digging two lakes

The Marquis of Dufferin and Ava's private avenue at Helen's Bay railway station, now a public footpath.

F DUFFERIN ESTATE

S IN HAND COLOURED YELLOW

in the demesne and creating a remarkable private avenue from the demesne through estate lands to the sea at Helen's Bay via the railway station. The landscape architect James Fraser is said to have drawn up a plan for the estate in the 1860s,[35] though it is apparent from Lord Dufferin's correspondence that he had an intimate knowledge of the grounds and a passion for landscaping. While away from Ireland in his career as a diplomat, Lord Dufferin sent regular written instructions to explain details of the tree planting and landscaping that he wanted, and he demanded regular reports of progress.[36]

A detailed work programme drawn up for Clandeboye in 1861 gives an indication of the extent of the works. Amongst other estate matters, it refers to sites for tree planting, where thinning was to be undertaken, woods requiring protection from rabbits, woods needing fencing and areas for replanting. Most of the sites mentioned in this document were outside the walled demesne, including 'large clumps of plantation to be laid down on the tops of all of the high hills seen from the drive to the sea, fenced round effectively, and planted with whins.'[37] These hill top plantations, together with shelter belts and wooded drives, transformed the extensive district between Clandeboye, Craigantlet and Helen's Bay into a very attractive patchwork of woodland and meadows. The plantings were predominantly of beech with varying amounts of other broadleaved species and some pines. A degree of formality was created along the drive to Helen's Bay by lining this woodland strip with spaced lime trees.[38] Following the fashion of the time, Lord Dufferin did want some exotic conifers in his land. Reference to this can be found in the work plan of 1861 which included an instruction that Mr Ferguson of the Belfast Botanic Garden should be sent details of the pinetum and asked for advice about its development.

Calcutta
January 7 1887

My Dear Howe

Please look at the enclosed passage which I have marked in McCulloch's letter. Over and over again I have told him that he was not to do any landscape gardening. He is an idiot about matters of the kind, as you can see from the way in which he speaks of having given a 'clean and neat' appearance to a wood, as if that were not just the kind of appearance a wood aught not to have. What is wanted in a wood is brushwood and not grass. Perhaps no harm may really be done, but I greatly doubt it, for during my absence before I found that he had gone and cut down a good many of the wild and straggly laurels and rhododendrons which I had remembered from a child. I have been constantly enjoining him not to meddle with the shrubberies or do any trimming or anything of the kind and I shall be much obliged to you if you will speak very sharply to him, and tell him that unless he chooses to obey me in this respect he can go about his business. I confined his operations in the woods and shrubberies to the cutting down of trees which were injurious to other trees, and the cutting of laurels which were preventing the growth of rhododendrons. If we do not take care, on coming home I shall find Clandeboye looking like a suburban villa.

Yours sincerely

Dufferin

Although Lord Dufferin spent much of his working life away from Clandeboye, it is apparent from this and other correspondence that he kept a close eye on the landscaping of his estate. In a subsequent letter Lord Dufferin wrote to his Agent Thomas Howe to say he was satisfied that McCulloch had just cut suckers.[39]

On the opposite shore of Belfast Lough, near the coast between Belfast and Carrickfergus, there was some planting well before the end of the 18th century. One early reference to this can be found in a complaint published in a newspaper in 1770 by Mr Stewart that hazel and young forest trees on Whitehouse farm had been damaged. Tree lists registered by tenants in the 1790s include planting at Throne, Mount Vernon, Rush Park and Rosebank (Whiteabbey) and other sites in the area were planted in the following decades.[40] There was also repeat planting at some locations, such as the property known as Solitude in north Belfast which was described in 1830 as being 'skirted with Forest Trees, 1000 of which are 45 years growth, 1200 are 18 years planted, mostly Larch Fir and estimated worth £500.'[41] Around this time trees also started to change the appearance of properties further along the coast, as noted by Samuel M'Skimin in his account of Carrickfergus of 1811.

Previous page: Map of Dufferin Estate lands c. 1901.
The woods, hilltop plantations and avenue through the estate lands to the coast are clearly illustrated.

That part of this district lying along the shore, exhibits an agreeable landscape, in consequence of numerous enclosures, clumps of trees, gentlemen's seats, and a pretty numerous population…

This country at present has but little timber, but planting is becoming frequent, within these few years many thousands of young trees have been planted in clumps and screens near the different gentlemen's seats. [42]

As the woods planted around Belfast developed there were sales of thinnings and sometimes advertisements for trees felled for timber,[43] though no evidence has been found of widespread clear felling. Even at Ormeau, where it has been suggested that Lord Donegall disposed of all the timber of useful size in the 1860s, there is good evidence that many tall trees were retained.[44] Some woods were however lost as the inexorable growth of the urban area resulted in farms and gardens becoming the sites of industry and high-density housing. The spread of factories into estate lands around Cave Hill in the second half of the 19th century was noted by one travel writer, who referred to villas with plantations 'mingling with the tall chimneys, large factories, and hamlets which skirt the shore'.[45] During the 19th century woodland owners around Belfast were also faced with some other difficulties, such as at Clandeboye where there was a report of malicious damage caused by woodland being set on fire, and on another occasion a forester had to be dismissed for corruption over the sale of timber.[46] Of greater concern for woodsmen were sporadic severe gales, the worst being the 'Big Wind' of the night of 6th January 1839. This devastated much of the British Isles including the woods at Belvoir Park, where it was reported that over 1,000 trees were blown down.[47] In another storm around 1895 there was considerable damage to the woods at Clandeboye, with the loss of trees near the house, in lower parts of the grounds and on higher land near Helen's Tower.[48]

Trees of crags, cliffs and gullies

In contrast to the good growing conditions of the lowlands, the hill slopes around Belfast are more exposed and have heavier soils that are sometimes waterlogged. However, the hill walker who today visits the steep-sided stream valleys and rocky hill slopes around the city will often find areas of semi-natural hazel woodland. Hazel woods with ash or sometimes oak and a diverse flora including bluebell, wood anemone and primrose occur on steep slopes throughout the region, including cliffs along the Antrim coast and Scrabo Hill by Newtownards. The distribution of this habitat and its good flora indicate that the hazel woods are long-established, most likely many hundreds of years old.

The earliest references found to these woods are the writings of Samuel M'Skimin, who in 1811 noted that there was whitethorn (hawthorn) and shrubs like hazel on the southern slopes of Knockagh and that Woodburn Glen had 'a profusion of natural shrubbery'.[49] The Ordnance Survey Letters of the 1830s gave a very similar picture of the area around Carrickfergus, referring to 'numerous and extensive patches of brushwood which are still to be found occupying the banks of the streams, the precipitous declivities and the rocky and irreclaimable districts' and describing the ground to the south of Knockagh hill as 'scrag of native woodland.'[50] The Ordnance Survey also gave a good description of what was clearly semi-natural woodland on the hill slopes above Belfast in County Antrim:

With the exception of the summit and mountainous north eastern side of the Cave Hill, remains of natural wood are to be found in the stunted brushwood which is scattered, though thinly, over all its waste and unreclaimed patches, but chiefly under the precipices and broken declivities of the Cave Hill and Carnmoney hill, and over the steep banks of the little ravines and water courses. Hazel is the prevailing wood, but oak, ash, holly and birch, beside numerous aged and large hawthorns, are the description found. The brushwood is very stunted, being eaten down by cattle, and is rapidly disappearing before the operations of the husbandman. [51]

Despite the work of the husbandman and his cattle, areas of hazel wood were to survive around Cave Hill (particularly at Hazelwood and near the Upper Cavehill Road) and on parts of the southern and eastern slopes of Carnmoney Hill. Elsewhere in the region, hazel woods remained on the steep slopes of Knockagh and on the other side of Belfast on the Castlereagh Hills in glens to the north of Dundonald and at the upper reaches of the Purdys Burn.[52]

Although growing conditions in these river valleys and hill slopes are poor, some were planted in the 19th century, as they presented land owners with a wonderful landscaped setting for creating dramatic woodland scenery. Colin Glen, on the slopes of the Belfast hills above Dunmurry, is the best known glen in the Belfast area and a colourful and rather exaggerated description from 1823 indicates that this valley was well wooded:

> The stream is shallow, but of considerable breadth, and this place certainly unites more natural, as well as artificial beauty, than any of the other mountain rivers. The banks on many occasions must be more than two hundred feet in height, overspread with young and flourishing trees. It is by far the most extensive plantation in the parish, and the view of this part of the glen from some elevated points is eminently beautiful. The high and shelving banks are covered with such a mass of leaves and branches, that the rivulet below seems embosomed in green.[53]

At this time Colin Glen was known particularly for its oak trees,[54] though there were probably also long-established areas of hazel and ash, particularly in the higher parts of the glen. Many trees were added by the McCance family, who had extensive landholdings in the area and registered the planting of nearly 25,000 trees in 1809 and 1810 (Appendix 3). In the mid 19th century there was additional planting higher up in the Belfast Hills, including around 50-70 acres planted on the top of Collin Mountain, well above the Glen. However, this exposed planting was not successful and was described in 1908 as having no timber value and comprising trees 'only 12 or 13 feet high and not more than the thickness of your leg.'[55]

Colin Glen by Andrew Nicholl, painted in the 1830s.

Across the city on the Castlereagh Hills, the sale of a farm at Cregagh in 1811 referred to 'a vast quantity of Forest Trees in the most thriving condition, partly occupying a romantic ravine on the side of Cregagh hill.' This was most likely a plantation and there are also records that the glen near the house at Lisnabreeny was planted in 1827 with a total of 3,800 larch, Scots pine, spruce and beech.[56] Today the house is Lagan College and this glen is known as Cregagh Glen.

Along the northern side of Belfast Lough many steep slopes and river valleys were planted. For example at Rathfern, on the eastern slopes of Carnmoney Hill, the planting of over 12,000 mixed deciduous and broadleaved trees was registered in 1854.[57] The nearby valley of the Three Mile Water became the site of a notable 19th Century wooded garden created by W. Valentine of Glenavna. Members of the Belfast Naturalists' Field Club who visited the area in 1867 noted a western red cedar with golden foliage (*Thuja plicata* 'Aurea'), Monterey cypress (*Cupressus macrocarpa*) and fir trees. The gardens also boasted an extraordinary fernery that particularly caught the eye of the members of the Club.

> It occupies a site of about fifty feet square, and is approached by a serpentine grotto; being the effect on entering that of a ruined abbey, where foliage supplanted drapery, and Nature triumphed over art…its shady nooks, and caverned recesses, refreshed by the spray of jets and fountains, and the falling water of its miniature cataract, make it the very home of ferns, lycopodiums, and mosses, which are here in endless variety…In the centre of the building is a unique fountain, called a 'ferndelabrum,' combining a jet d'eau with convenient nitches for growing ferns…[58]

Hazel with an understorey of wood anemone, primrose and wood-rush at Cave Hill.

Late 19th century photograph of the Hermitage, Glenavna.

Victorians were drawn towards these romantic landscapes and, in addition to the grotto, a second rustic structure was constructed by the Three Mile Water, a timber hideaway called the Hermitage. A painting of Colin Glen by Belfast artist Andrew Nicholl dating from the 1830s shows that in this wooded valley a similar rustic structure (a 'moss house') was erected.[59] In yet another steep-sided valley, south Woodburn Glen in the hills above Carrickfergus, the Belfast Water Commissioners created an enchanting footpath that followed the edge of the stream, crisscrossing on a series of little bridges to a waterfall known as the Grey Mare's Tail. This was finished in time to provide an attraction for delegates attending the 1874 meeting of the British Association in Belfast.[60]

Cave Hill

In the early part of the 19th century perpetual leases were granted for much of the extensive Donegall landholdings and the family retained for their own use only two areas, their house and demesne at Ormeau and the Deer Park at Cave Hill.[61] These lands were the private shooting grounds for the second Marquis, who employed both a park keeper and gamekeeper at the Deer Park.[62]

We know from the writings of the naturalist William Thompson that there were fallow deer grazing in the park on Cave Hill in the early 19th century[63] though by this time the trees that had once shaded the Deer Park had been felled (see Chapter 3) and this must have been an exposed location. There are also references to deer in the correspondence of the third Marquis of Donegall from the late 1840s to the early 1850s. In these letters the Marquis wrote to his agent in Belfast about the need for winter feeding, for housing (he suggested taking trees from Ormeau to make huts in the park) and for care in slaughtering. He took great pride in his herd, giving directions for venison to be given to his friends and in 1849 for a buck to be sent onboard the Royal Yacht when Queen Victoria visited Belfast.[64]

When in 1854 the Marquis was approached to sell the Cave Hill Deer Park to provide a site for a public cemetery he declined the offer, explaining in a letter to his agent that he didn't want to part with 'the only little bit of land I can really call my own.'[65] However in January 1859 notices appeared for the sale of the herd, comprising 15 bucks, 50 does and about 25 fawns.[66] This marked the end of deer keeping on Cave Hill, a tradition that had lasted for over 150 years. Keeping a herd would have been very expensive and this may have been a necessary cost-cutting exercise, though the sale was probably also prompted by new plans that were being developed for this historic site.

On the 22nd of November 1864 the Belfast News-Letter noted that the Marquis of Donegall was proposing to build a family residence on Cave Hill. Construction started around 1868 and just three years later the mansion was nearing completion.[67] This building, which today is still one of the most imposing in the city, became known as Belfast Castle. With the deer gone, the former grazed grasslands could be planted and large tracts of the Deer Park and most of the adjacent slopes of Cave Hill were used to create the largest upland wood in the Belfast area. The first note found for the delivery of trees was for evergreen oaks supplied in October 1869.[68] Rabbits, which can seriously damage young plantations, were culled and later, as the new woodlands developed, pheasant were introduced.[69] There were a number of periods of planting in the latter part of the 19th century, predominantly of broadleaved trees including beech, sycamore, elm and lime, but also areas of larch, Scots pine and Norway spruce. Two Scots pine growing at the top of the woodland by the path to the caves, recently tree-ring dated, have given start dates of 1896 and 1904 and it is thought that the conifers planted as specimen trees by Belfast Castle also date from this period.[70]

Late 19th century photograph of Belfast Castle. At this time a belt of woodland had been planted at the foot of the cliffs, but towards the mansion house there were only scattered bushes.

A snapshot of plant material purchased for Cave Hill is given in an estate cash book for 1897. This lists payments for trees and shrubs that would have been planted on the hill slopes, plants for the vegetable gardens and flowers and roses that were probably for setting out in beds near the mansion house. More puzzling to explain are two purchases of a total of 3,000 St. Johns Wort. This plant was perhaps chosen to add colour along the fringes of the new woodlands. Most of the trees and plants were from English suppliers, though roses were ordered from the Belmont nursery of Hugh Dixon.[71]

March 16 1897	*Laurels and other shrubs*..	*£70 10s 6d*
March 16 1897	*Sycamore Elm for £49 10s 0d and £1 18s 3d*	*£51 8s 3d*
April 2 1897	*Beech trees for £22 15s 6d and 3s 6d*...	*£22 19s*
May 26 1897	*Rhododendrons Laurels Larch Spruce firs*..	*£11 15s*
May 26 1897	*Mountain Ash Beech Japonica*	*£35 6s 6d*

Payments made for trees and shrubs supplied 1896-1897 for Belfast Castle Estate.[71]

6. Trees and parks for the people

Belfast still had a small population at the beginning of the 19th century, though the rate of growth had started to become noticeable. In 1827 one older resident wrote to the local newspaper to comment about the development of Belfast. He was proud that visitors now arrived by steam navigation and could be shown the new gasworks and college, though he decried the way the town he knew as a child was changing. It was no longer possible to show all the sights of Belfast from the vantage point of the top of the Poorhouse (now Clifton House).

> *Some twenty years ago, my task was an easy one, and I generally satisfied my companions' curiosity by conducting them to the Poor-House steeple and shewing them our compact little town lying before us, and the Lagan winding in the distance. Now-a-days, things are changed; people have got the building mania, and the town has broke loose, extending beyond its ancient limits, and engrossing all the town parks and neat gardens that I remember when a boy.[1]*

During the Victorian period Belfast was to develop increasingly quickly, and with this growth there was increasing need for public open space. Access was permitted to the grounds of a few of the big houses, such as the Cultra and Ballymenoch Demesnes near Holywood, which one writer in 1825 noted with satisfaction had been 'thrown open without reserve or distinction.'[2] Dedicated public spaces were created, initially the Botanic Garden at Stranmills, followed by Queen's Island in the harbour. There were also some short-lived attempts to create places for public recreation within the town.[3] The first public park was at Ormeau, which was initially known as the 'People's Park' a title that distinguished it from the private parks of the gentry. By the time Belfast became a city in 1888 the desire to create attractive public spaces had quite literally moved on to the streets, with the Corporation organising tree planting along pavements.

Belfast Botanic Garden

The first steps in the development of a botanic garden for Belfast date from 1827 when a small area of land near the town was rented and a gardener was employed. The Belfast News-Letter avidly reported the arrival of collections of seeds and plants. Material came from locations as dispersed as the West Indies, Germany, the Cape of Good Hope and Madagascar. To maximise interest, the News-Letter article also included a list of many exotic-sounding plants and trees from far-flung countries which *may* have been represented in the collections.[4]

At a meeting in January 1828 the Belfast Botanic and Horticultural Society was formed and a permanent home for the Botanic Garden was identified at Portview House and farm in south Belfast. This had previously been the site of John Bullen's nursery. The house and land was in a neglected state though it had the advantages of an attractive setting and mature trees, and trustees of the society signed a lease of the land from the Marquis of Donegall (who became president of the society) for 999 years.[5] A circular was printed to set out the merits of the venture. The Garden was to be a place where new ideas in agriculture and gardening could be tested and the biological sciences promoted. It was also proposed to be a resort for taking the air, for exercise and for an agreeable walk.[6] Judging by an editorial in the Northern Whig newspaper, some anticipated that the venture would encourage even higher ideals:

> *We cannot dismiss this brief notice, without wishing the Botanic Garden every success. Our juvenile friends (of both sexes) will find the science of Botany a study replete with instruction and delight. There is something in it, which makes the heart of man better and purer; which estranges him from the grosser pursuits of life, and leads him, as it were, by a chain of flowers, into a train of reflections which must bring his mind into closer connexion with the views and plans of his bounteous Creator.[7]*

However, despite the enthusiasm and optimism of the founders, in 1838 just 10 years after the formation of the Society, the committee reported that the Garden might have to close if there was not more public support.[8] Thankfully, this warning seems to have revitalised the committee. A Coronation Fete was held to raise funds and to encourage interest in local flora the 'Templeton Prize' (named after John Templeton, the Belfast botanist) was awarded for the display of rare native plants in pots. A four-year gardening apprenticeship scheme was set up under the charge of the Curator. Also, most significantly, a start was

made to develop what was to become the jewel of the Garden, the magnificent Palm House.[9]
Trees formed an important part of the Botanic Garden. As early as 1830 it was reported that preparations were being made for the planting of an arboretum and in 1837 there was mention of two donations of willows, 100 species from the Duke of Bedford and 72 species from Glasnevin.[10] By the time that a guide to the Botanic Garden was published in 1851 there was a pinetum and collections of horse chestnuts, maples, hawthorns, elms, willows and oaks.[11]

The situation in which are planted the conifera, struck us when we first saw it, as being particularly adapted to this family: in soil, shelter, and partial shade, the health of the plants and the shoots they have made, confirm our first impression; we may notice the following as striking for the time they have been planted :- Pinus Montezuma, 3 feet high, excelsa, Lambertiana, Gerardiana, macrophylla, 3 feet, apulcensis, Sabiniana, 5 feet; Coulteri, 6 feet (very fine); Pallasiana, uncinata, Devoniana, Hartwegi, filifolia, insignis and Auracaria imbricata, 5 feet; nor is Cedrus deodara or Abes Douglasi, any thing behind them. (Farmer's Gazette, 1845)

The pines are all planted singly, and in slight groups on the lawn, each tree standing on a small grassy mound, and at a respectable distance from each other, even where they are formed into groups.
The following are about the heights of a few of the finest specimens of the Coniferae :- Cupressus macrocarpa, or Lambert's large-coned Cypress, a beautiful tree, 12 feet in height; the upright Arborvitae (Thuja stricta), 7 feet high; Taxodium distichum, or Deciduous Cypress, an exceedingly handsome tree 22 feet in height; Norman's Silver Fir (Abies Nordmanniana), 2½ feet high, and 3 feet diameter, an exceedingly beautiful specimen; Douglas's Spruce (Abies Douglasii), 20 feet in height; a beautiful little specimen of the Oriental Spruce (Abies orientalis), an inhabitant of the coast of the Black Sea and adjacent mountains to the east, attracted our attention by its handsome form, and short, thick, palid, green leaves; the Himalayan Spruce (Abies Morinda) a fine plant, was 10 feet high, and finely branched; Montezuma's Pine (Pinus Montezumae), 10 feet in height: Coulter's Pine (Pinus Coulteri), 25 feet; Hook-coned Pine (Pinus uncinata), 18 feet, said to be the finest of the sort in that part of the country; Black Austrian Pine (Pinus Austriaca) 16 feet; the Remarkable Pine (Pinus insignis) a fine specimen, about 12 feet in height…The straight-leaved Pine (Pinus macrophylla), 16 feet in height; and many other fine specimens, such as the Picea Pinsapo and Araucaria imbricata, two magnificent plants of which grace the smooth lawn between the principal walk and the chief range of plant houses. One of these Araucarias is 16 feet in height, the other not quite so tall. They are very regularly branched, stretching their decumbent arms over the smooth turf. (The Scottish Gardener, 1854).

Victorians were fascinated by the ever increasing diversity of conifers that were being introduced and the collection in the Belfast Botanic Garden attracted the attention of two visitors who not only provided lists of Latin names but also measured these trees.[12]

Unlike most of the comparable institutions in Britain and Ireland, the Belfast Botanic Garden received no support from government and for income relied largely on shareholders and members who paid an annual subscription. The general public were only permitted admission to special events. In 1840 and again in 1848 for trial periods the Garden was made available to all for a few hours each Saturday on the payment of a small charge.[13] However, despite the need to generate more income and lobbying for greater access by a group called the Working Classes' Association,[14] there were concerns expressed about opening the gates to the 'operative classes'.

In an attempt to find a solution to the twin issues of access and finance a fund was set up in 1865 to provide for free admission on Saturday afternoons.[15] Money was also increasingly generated from activities that appealed to something less than the values advocated by the founders. Balloon ascents became regular public spectacles. In 1851 crowds were attracted by a display of war dances by Zulu chiefs. Some years there were sports and circus acts, particularly on Easter Monday when between the trees and flower beds could be seen Roman chariot races, a clown attempting to drive four geese in a washing tub through the lake and 'Ohmy, the flying man.'[16]

Visitors to the Botanic Garden invariably noted with pleasure the appearance of the grounds. However, by the beginning of the last decade of the century public events were failing to generate much profit and the financial situation was described at one meeting as being 'rather precarious'. The original aims of the Garden were also not being met, a Director noting that it was not of use to students of Queen's

Botanic Gardens Belfast.

University studying botany. There were ominous discussions about selling land to raise capital.[17] Other fund-raising ideas such as attracting visitors by developing the botanical collections, increasing sales of cut plants and flowers and encouraging more subscriptions were discussed, but without much optimism that they would provide a solution.[18] In 1894, an approach was made to Belfast Corporation for the Garden to be taken over as a public park.[19]

Queen's Island

Queen's Island originated from an engineering project to improve access to the docks at Belfast by straightening the channel at the mouth of the River Lagan. Work commenced in 1839 and the excavated material was used to form an area of raised ground in the tidal mudflats. Part of this new island was used for harbour facilities and towards the Lough a battery of eight guns was installed, though much of the land was landscaped to create promenades by constructing paths and planting trees and shrubs. The island was used as a vantage point when Queen Victoria visited Belfast on board the Royal Yacht in 1849 and in the following year a fete was held at the site to commemorate the occasion and to raise funds for the General Hospital.[20]

The organising committee developed ambitious plans for the erection of a 'Crystal Palace', inspired by the much larger building of the same name created for the Great Exhibition in Hyde Park in London and a single-storey structure of glass, iron and wood was constructed remarkably quickly during 1851. At the triumphal opening the design of the building was praised and it was claimed that the architect, Mr John Boyd, had improved on the design of the London Palace.[21] Events held on Queen's Island in 1851 included a display of fireworks and regatta, a Victoria bazaar and a 'fete for the working classes' with an exhibition of highland dancing and popular sports including running, leaping and sack races, climbing soaped poles, chasing greased pigs and women's punt races.[22]

There were discussions about reserving land at Queen's Island as a public park[23] and although the aspiration was never fully realised, this landscaped site became a popular focus for attractions, sports and games. The Crystal Palace provided an extensive covered space that included a fountain with a statue of

Neptune, plants and by the late 1850s, a small zoo.[24] Queen's Island competed with the Botanic Garden as a venue for public events, and this competition must have become more intense when, in 1863, the Palace on Queen's Island was rented and laid out with botanical displays.

Amongst the recent additions are peaches, plums, pears, apples, cherries, figs, and white currants (all in pots), fine specimens of the tea-tree, the New Zealand flax, the coffee-tree, the banyan-tree, and about a hundred varieties of new roses. The name, in Latin and English, is attached to each of the plants, and this will very much assist the visitors. It should be mentioned, further, that the conservatory contains the largest specimen of the Acaccia tree in Ireland, and that it is now covered with blooms. The whole interior of the Palace has undergone a complete renovation, and the varied contents are laid out with great good taste.[25]

However, access to the island was a problem particularly during popular Easter events, with overcrowded boats and reports of people falling in the water.[26] In 1864 a fire badly damaged the Palace and plans to restore it came to nothing. The presence of a pleasure garden in a developing port also must have become increasingly inappropriate. Amusements and band performances continued to be held for a number of years, though Queen's Island was last the scene of public events in the late 1870s.[27]

BIRD'S EYE VIEW OF BELFAST.

Belfast in 1863. The Queen's Island pleasure grounds can be seen at the mouth of the Lagan on the near (County Down) side of the river.

Public parks

The lobbying for access to the Botanic Garden by the Working Classes' Association was part of a wider campaign for public open space for the growing population of Belfast. A People's Park Committee was formed. A paper advocating parks and criticising the enclosure of open spaces was delivered to the Belfast Social Inquiry Society in 1852 by James Thomson.[28] A series of newspaper articles by Reverend O'Hanlon which were published as a book in 1853 condemned the squalid and unhealthy conditions of the poor in the rapidly growing town. He argued for the establishment of a park 'for the recreation and health of our pent-up population' or at least greater access to the Botanic Garden and the grounds of the Waterworks on the Antrim Road.[29] In the summer of 1855 a plan to open the Waterworks on Sundays as a public promenade was vigorously debated and crowds that gathered at the gates demanding greater access even forced an entry.[31] Further pressure for public open space was generated when an established path to Cave Hill was blocked by a landowner. This resulted in the formation of an Association for the Protection of Public Rights of Way and to a court case in 1859 which asserted the right of access.[32]

Here, as I beheld the dense population, and felt the atmosphere, like a leaden weight, and looked at wan mothers, and sickly, emaciated children all around, it occurred to me to ask if these poor creatures ever breathe God's pure air, or look at nature, out amid fields, and trees, and hedgerows? The inquiries, though made in the least sentimental fashion, only extorted smiles – ghastly smiles, indeed. They never think of such things. If they could only satisfy their hunger, and get something in the shape of clothing for themselves and their children, they would be content to forget that nature consisted of anything else than those dark, dingy brick walls, built up there so close together that it might seem to have been the design of the architect to shut out both light and air; they know nothing of the pure breath of heaven which comes over hill and dale, redolent of health and fragrance; 'they live where they are, and they are used to it' – yes; used, by day and by night, to inhale a putrid atmosphere, which is death – slow it may be, but certain death. 'When,' said I, to a withered, sallow, sunken man, old in constitution, but as to years only in the prime of life, 'when did you last see a green field?' 'About six months ago, when I went to the railway,' was his reply. Is Belfast, with its one hundred and four thousand inhabitants, not able or willing to provide a park for its soiled and alley-living population – to which they might be won, and where they might learn the value of God's sunshine and air, and get a glimpse of nature in her genial and soul-reviving forms?

'Walks amongst the poor of Belfast' by Reverend W. M. O'Hanlon, published in 1853.[30]

Plans for a permanent park that would be open to all took a step forward when the Harbour Commissioners sought to extend the port by reclaiming tidal land on the County Down side of the Lough and, as part of this development, agreed that 50 acres at Ballymacarrett would be set aside for public open space.[33] The decision to develop this site, to be known as Victoria Park, appears to have been on the understanding that Queen's Island would eventually lose its pleasure grounds. Plans for Victoria Park were

Looking towards the city from south of the Ormeau Bridge by Hugh Thompson c. 1880. When Ormeau Park was opened in 1871, it was noted with concern that the site was outside Belfast and when this view was painted the area still had a rural aspect. Today it is thought of as being close to the heart of the city.

72

widely publicised when in 1855 representatives of the People's Park Committee made an address to the Lord Lieutenant.[34] However progress was slow. In part this was because of difficulties in providing access,[35] and it was also an unpromising site - one commentator referred to the land as a 'mud-enclosed slob' and suggested that it should be sold for oyster farming![36]

The possibility of creating another area of public open space arose in 1864 when there were discussions about purchasing Ormeau Demesne from the Marquis of Donegall for a People's Park and also a cemetery. A valuation was undertaken of the land but no agreement was reached.[37] In the following year the Corporation formed a sub-committee which started to investigate the powers needed to create public parks.[38] There was pressure to move quickly as at the time the Marquis of Donegall was considering disposing of Ormeau for a housing development and building his new mansion in the Cave Hill Deer Park.[39] However, after the passing of the Public Parks (Ireland) Act in 1869, the demesne lands at Ormeau were acquired for Belfast's first park, which opened in 1871.[40]

Now that Belfast had a park, the laying out of Ormeau had to be considered. It was initially proposed to employ a landscape gardener, but this was rejected by the Town Council and it was decided that a plan could be obtained through a public competition with a prize of £100.[41] Unfortunately this proved to be a mistake as, when the submissions were examined, it was found that none met the specified requirements. One problem was that the submissions did not deal effectively with a requirement for housing development on part of the site to generate income to create the park. Some of the proposals were also excessive and impractical. For example, Mr J. F. Johnson (the curator of the Botanic Garden) submitted a plan that included a tower that would send jets of water into lakes linked by steams with cascades. He also added in his plan five park entrances, nine bridges and a windmill by the Lagan to drain low-lying land.[42] In the end a finalist was selected by a series of ballots, and the award was made, though this was on the condition that the winning plan did not have to be adopted.[43]

Once the distraction caused by the prize competition had been resolved, the Parks Committee was able to move forward. The Borough Surveyor drew up a plan for housing on the periphery of Ormeau and in January 1874 the post of superintendent was advertised at a salary of £100 a year plus accommodation, the post holder to be skilled in landscape gardening.[44] A general plan was developed and work commenced. Benches and swings were installed and sites for croquet and cricket were laid out.[45] Colourful shrubs were purchased from the nursery of Mr Mann of Poyntzpass including 100 variegated holly, 100 English yew, 50 pampas grass, 100 *Arbutus*, 100 *Aucuba japonica*, 50 variegated 'tree box', 100 *Berberis darwinii*, and a few specimen trees. Another order for the park was for 200 rhododendron.[46] Gifts for the new public park included deer, which were contained using hurdles and later wrought iron fencing. However, Ormeau would not have resembled a typical deer park as for a while the deer grazed alongside three donated emu.[47]

Despite the difficulties encountered in creating public spaces, pressure for more parks was unrelenting. While the fledgling Parks Committee was trying to resolve the issues of laying out Ormeau, they were also responding to a desire to create another public space at Falls. The proposed site was surplus land that had been acquired as part of a new cemetery project by the Falls Road. Although there was a need to amend the Parks Act as the land was outside the borough, the project was supported by an active local committee and Falls Park opened just five years after Ormeau, in 1876.[48] Planting at this new park included 1,500 trees 'of the Austrian pine, larch and fir description' ordered by the Town Clerk in 1884. Falls Park was probably also the destination for 100 variegated hollies purchased by the Parks Committee in 1879 from Van Tol and Van Kleef of Holland 'at £6 delivered at Belfast Quay. Cost Freight and Insurance'.[49]

As Belfast continued to expand during the late Victorian period - the housing stock quadrupled between 1870 and 1900 - the move to create public parks continued to grow and by the end of the century Alexandra, Woodvale and Dunville Parks had also been opened. The future of the Botanic Garden was secured when Belfast Corporation took over the site in 1895 and renamed it the Belfast Botanic Gardens Park. Victoria Park was finally opened in 1906.[50]

This early postcard of Duncairn Gardens, Antrim Road, shows an abundance of street trees. Some of the trees are well established and in leaf. Others, which must have been recently planted, are supported by stakes and are bare.

Early street tree planting

Residents of the Belfast area in the 19th century would have been accustomed to seeing avenues of trees in private estates and, where leases stipulated the planting of spaced timber trees like oak, ash and beech in hedgerows, these would have formed rows of tall trees along country roads. However the planting of street trees in Belfast does not seem to have developed as the result of a corporation policy or public campaign, but slowly evolved in the latter part of the 19th century, as part of the programme of road widening undertaken by the Belfast Corporation Improvement Committee.

Initially trees were probably only planted by the Improvement Committee to compensate for those removed in widening schemes. For example the Committee minutes from 1874 recorded that a tree by the Wesleyan (Methodist) College that was obstructing the thoroughfare was to be removed and two years later the Surveyor was instructed to plant six new trees with guards by the College.[51] Before long street tree planting was being undertaken across the city. For example, in 1886 the Surveyor was asked to plant 12 or 14 trees on Clifton Street and in the following year to plant trees on Stranmillis Road and fix guards on two trees on the Crumlin Road.[52] Details of the species planted were seldom recorded but most were probably lime and London plane, the latter being frequently used in cities, because it was considered to be pollution resistant.

As interest in street tree planting grew, the Improvement Committee started to receive requests from residents. When there was a lack of funds a do-it-yourself approach was on occasions advocated, such as when residents of Glenravel Street asked for trees and were informed that spaces could be left in the pavement if they undertook the planting.[53] In University Street, a partnership approach was used: the street trees were paid for by the owners of the properties and the Improvement Committee provided tree guards and arranged for the Surveyor to organise the planting.[54] Developers sometimes planted trees when they laid out new streets, though their work was scrutinised by the Committee. When builders H. & J. Martin planted trees along North Parade, they were informed that unless the Superintendent of Ormeau Park was satisfied that the trees were properly planted and had been provided with drains and guards to the satisfaction of the Surveyor, they would have to be removed.[55]

The involvement of Parks staff in the planting along North Parade was not an isolated occurrence. In 1886 the Surveyor was instructed to remove dead trees in Dublin Road and other places and to plant replacements supplied by Wm. Dickson the Parks Superintendent.[56] In 1900 the Improvement Committee made an official request to involve the Cemetery and Parks Committee in street tree planting[57] and the sharing of responsibilities between two committees was subsequently raised in the minutes on a number of occasions. However this was never a satisfactory arrangement, and remained an impediment until local government reorganisation in the second half of the following century.

Slate roofs and chimneys dominate in this unusual late 19th century view of the centre of Belfast. The tall structure in the middle distance is Robinson & Cleaver's building. The City Hall, which today stands opposite, had not been built when this photograph was taken. The wide road on the left is Chichester Street, along which street trees can be seen.

7. Decades of neglect

Despite the extensive tree planting undertaken during much of the 19th century, a report of a government committee into Irish forestry of 1908 made depressing reading. It found that up to 1880 the rate of planting in Ireland had exceeded felling but that subsequently, and particularly during the period 1880 to 1891, the trend had reversed. In addition, it was noted that the best woods were being felled, leading to a deterioration in woodland quality. This situation was a consequence of Land Acts that had resulted in the break up of estates. Landowners found that plantations were an obstacle to the sale of land and, as there was also increasing demand for timber, woods were felled. When tenants acquired land that had been planted they often sold the trees as they had little interest in forestry and felling provided income.[1]

This gloomy picture helped prompt the development of state forestry in rural areas, but no particular measures were taken by government to promote urban trees. In the Belfast region the owners of the large estates stopped creating large scale woods and after the First World War many of the large mansions and their grounds were in a state of decline. The Depression, Second World War and lack of planning control also impacted on the urban environment. In the 25 years from 1926 to 1951 the amount of open space in the county borough of Belfast more than halved and woodland decreased from 2.5% to 1.3% of land area.[2]

There were, thankfully, a few environmental schemes in Belfast that went against this trend. The most significant was a new approach to city living that, for a short period at the beginning of the 20th century, did much to encourage tree planting in streets, gardens and open spaces. Another development worthy of note was the laying out of the landscaped grounds at the Parliament Building at Stormont, which was completed by the early 1930s. However, it was not until the 1970s that interest in enhancing the urban environment would slowly start to return.

Suburban trees and gardens

The Garden City movement had developed in the 1890s in England in response to the unplanned, overcrowded and unsanitary conditions of Victorian industrial cities and proposed planned, self-contained communities. The approach was soon taken up in Belfast and advertisements appeared for garden suburbs. These were schemes of distinctive, affordable houses with spacious gardens along tree-lined roads. The language used by the developers promoted the healthy environment and natural beauty and setting of the sites. These homes were away from the dirt and smoke of the city and often close to a park, golf course, the countryside and the new electric tram routes.

The Suburban Colony Company Ltd developed a number of sites around Belfast, the first at Downshire off the Cregagh Road, which in 1905 was proudly announced to be the first 'garden colony' in County Down. In a promotional article it was stated that representatives of the company had visited many of the English and continental cities 'most remarkable for the beauty and "up to dateness" of their ideas' including

Hampton Park, Ormeau Road. These trees, like many of the older street trees have a mass of slender branches growing from the top of the trunk, evidence that they were formerly pollarded, a labour intensive method of pruning.

Port Sunlight and Letchworth. The houses were to be of artistic construction; 'each and all enable the occupier to be the tiller of his own soil, to enjoy an interesting and healthy pastime, and to supply the necessities of his household in the matter of fruit, flowers, and vegetables.'[3]

Around the same time the Belfast Garden Company developed sites at Cliftonville, Ravenhill Park and Saint James's Park off the Donegall Road. The most ambitious of these was at Cliftonville, which it was stated fulfilled all the requirements of a garden city and yet was close to the penny tram and only ten minutes from the city centre. A competition was held to promote housing of good but economical design, and building took place in the area bounded by Cliftonville and Westland Roads. Each house was to be individually designed and with a garden described as commodious. Here, the company said, children could play in comfort and free from risks. Vegetables, plants and flowers could be cultivated 'removed from the noise and bustle and smoke of the town, and with picturesque surroundings of the most diversified character.'[4] Street trees were planted, a pleasure garden with a tea house and a bowling green were proposed, where in the summertime band performances, concerts and games would be held. It was said that 100,000 shrubs, flowers and trees would be planted and the streets were to be called Aster, Begonia, Daffodil, Hollyhock and Fern Gardens.[5] Unfortunately the community facilities did not last and more traditional street names were chosen, though attention was paid to landscaping. Street trees were planted in all of the housing sites and fruit trees that until recent years were a common sight in the back gardens in places such as Cliftonville and Ravenhill Park were most likely provided by the company.[6]

Belfast Garden Company development at Cliftonville, junction of Kelvin Parade and Cardigan Drive.
The wide range of house styles and closely spaced street trees are a notable feature of this early 20th century postcard.

The garden city movement influenced the development of the Purdysburn Asylum, which was created in the demesne of the Purdysburn Estate (purchased by Belfast Corporation in 1894), and adjacent farm land. What was called a 'villa colony' of attractive redbrick buildings was constructed in extensive landscaped grounds that included woods, wilderness areas and agricultural land. The patients were encouraged to help in workshops, use the grounds for exercise and recreation and spend part of the day working in the asylum farm, which provided their food. The author of a newspaper article of 1910 was impressed by the layout of the buildings. 'Instead of being huddled behind forbidding walls, they are screened by belts of fir trees and beeches, and look out across green fields and brown furrows to a hillside ablaze with furze blossoms.' The writer went on to comment that 'the idea of an asylum never enters one's mind, the suggestion is rather of the newest experiment in garden cities'.[7]

The same ideals inspired an extensive landscaped garden at a food-processing factory that opened at Newforge by the bank of the River Lagan in 1928. There was no housing associated with the factory but the extensive grounds were laid out with lawns, flower beds and trees. Walks and a tennis court were constructed and staff and local residents were encouraged to treat the grounds as a community facility. The industrial buildings were integrated into the surroundings and nearby farmland used to grow crops for products canned at the factory.[8] The founder of the business, Robert Clement Wilson, took a close personal interest in the project and after the factory shut was keen that the grounds remained a public space. Today, this riverside land is Clement Wilson Park.

Probably because trees and gardens were now seen as part of city life, during the early years of the 20th century the Belfast Corporation Improvement Committee received an increasing number of requests for street tree planting, and there is abundant evidence that these trees were valued by residents. For example in 1901 when a landowner in Parkmount Avenue asked for a number of street trees to be removed to facilitate a property development, a delegation came to the Improvement Committee to protest. A letter written to the Evening Telegraph in 1906 indicated even stronger support for planting along pavements. At Donegall Avenue trees described as 'putting out their tender and beautiful foliage' had been snapped by vandals and the writer suggested that citizens should appoint themselves as special constables to try to prevent damage to street trees. In 1908 the Improvement Committee received a letter from Miss Mary Thompson of University Street asking for information on street tree planting and offering to pay for an oak for the pavement opposite her residence. Remarkably, this letter prompted the setting up of a sub-committee to look into the subject and, as a result, a more strategic programme was developed. Priority was given to planting on main routes, with a budget of £100 set aside for trees along the Antrim, Donegall, Falls and Shankill Roads, though planting in some other suburban streets continued and what was described as a suitable tree was planted by Mary Thompson's house.[9]

Trees, Wellington Park.
Councillor Wheeler attended to support the application to have trees planted in the footways of Wellington Park, and Alderman Sir Otto Jaffe and Councillor R. Johnson attended for a similar purpose. The Surveyor submitted an amended estimate, which showed the cost of planting trees 50 feet apart to be £45, and it was
Moved by Councillor Shaw,
Seconded by Councillor Irvine, and
Resolved – That the Surveyor be instructed to have the planting of the trees carried out by contract, and to arrange that payment therefor be deferred until after 1st April next.

Councillors were often keen to support tree planting. Minute of the Town Improvement Committee of 12 October 1909.[10]

Unfortunately, this enthusiasm for urban improvement did not last. Scant attention was paid to parks during the First World War or in the following two decades which were marked by a lack of urban growth and the economic collapse of the 1930s. Street tree planting was all but forgotten until a resurgence towards the end of the century. Developers lost interest in the environment of the city. Cliftonville's aspiration to be a part of the garden city movement withered away, and by the 1940s was only occasionally referred to by those who lived in the area, and then 'with a sort of affectionate irony.'[11]

Decline of the private estate

Political, social and financial pressures following the First World War had a major impact on the large landowners, who had little incentive to enhance estate grounds or to plant trees. Some large houses near Belfast were acquired for new uses and their grounds were preserved. One such example was Stranmillis House, which became a teacher training college in 1922, and most of the surrounding woods, gardens and lawns were retained and enhanced by grounds staff with the help of students.[12] Some other estate lands in the Belfast area were developed into golf courses, and at these sites old parkland trees and areas of woodland were generally kept to enhance the fairways. Clandeboye survived, though parts of the estate

The mansion house at Belvoir Park in decay. It was demolished in 1961.

had to be sold, trees were cut for timber and the house became dilapidated.[13] Other historic demesnes - including Belvoir Park and Belfast Castle, which were amongst the largest and most impressive in the Belfast area - were threatened with development and the obliteration of their long established landscapes.

The mansion at Belvoir Park was last occupied in 1925 after which the demesne woodlands and gardens were unmanaged. Part of the demesne was used to create the 18-hole Belvoir Golf Club which opened in 1929, and in 1934 the mansion and the remainder of the demesne, together with other estate farm lands, were sold to a development company. This company proposed to build what one commentator said would be 'the greatest building development ever undertaken in Ireland.' However the depressed state of the housing market in the 1930s and 1940s and the introduction of planning regulations that sought to protect the Lagan Valley thankfully prevented the destruction of this important old woodland and parkland.[14]

The mansion at Cave Hill, Belfast Castle, was last lived in during the 1920s, less than 60 years after it had been built. In 1933 there was a proposal for the entirety of the Belfast Castle Demesne to be developed, a newspaper article indicating that land would be 'given over to the woodsman's axe and to the road-makers, and the clang of the trowel will ring out where once one could hear alone the song of the birds.'[15] Fortunately only the lower slopes were built on and, in 1934, the Castle and the rest of the estate land, which included much of the former deer park, was acquired by Belfast Corporation and became a public park.[16]

One notable exception to the decline of the big estate arose from the need for suitable accommodation for the new Northern Ireland administration. For the new Parliament Building impressive landscaped grounds were laid out at Stormont. The Stormont Estate was developed from an initial purchase in December 1921 of the Victorian Stormont Castle and slightly over 235 acres of land, including 100 acres of woodland, from the Cleland family. Parliament Building was designed by Arnold Thornley, who also prepared drawings for a Processional Avenue to the Upper Newtownards Road. In 1928 Mr W. J. Bean, Curator of Kew Gardens, was invited to visit the site and provide advice about the landscaping. Initially it was suggested that the Processional Avenue should be lined with rows of elm, though it was subsequently decided to plant red-twigged lime.[17]

The Processional Avenue at Stormont in 2008.

NORTHERN IRELAND HOUSES OF PARLIAMENT, BELFAST.

By the time that Parliament Building was officially opened in November 1932, the avenues of limes had been laid out and rows of Irish yew planted in front of the Parliament Building. On the advice of Mr Bean, belts of woodland and copses were developed on either side of the Avenue with a mixture of deciduous species including colourful trees such as copper beech, *Sorbus* and laburnum on the woodland edges. Pines were chosen to enhance two small hills and in a wetter part of the grounds poplar, willow and alder were planted.

The proposed planting of the Processional Avenue was first mentioned in Public Record Office files on 28th May 1928, by the Governor (Duke of Abercorn). The architect Sir Arnold Thornley drew up plans for the planting of the two double rows of Red Twigged Lime trees (Tilia platyphyllos Rubra) on either side of the Prince of Wales Avenue. He arranged the spacing so that the lines of trees were not parallel, but diverged from 200 feet (61m) at the entrance to 250 feet (76 m) at the upper end, thus creating a false perspective.

Mr D. Stewart, Forestry Officer (Ministry of Agriculture) was required to provide estimates for the costs of ground preparation and planting. The preparatory work mainly involved soiling and excavation and in some areas levels had to be raised due to poor drainage. These mounds are still apparent up to 12 feet in diameter. Mr Stewart located a supply of 80 suitable Lime trees at Alex Dickson's Nursery at Newtownards, but these had a degree of root damage from lifting and he asked that they be left to stand a further year. In the meantime HM Office of Works located a supply in England, which were purchased in April 1929.

Planting the Avenue began on 25th November 1929 at a spacing of 80 feet (24.4m) between the trees in each row. Due to re-grading and settlement of the upper section, planting was not completed until 16th February 1932. In the meantime, Arnold Thornley formed the opinion that the trees were too far apart and on his recommendation, trees were planted midway between the initial planting, resulting in the present spacing of 40 feet (12.2m) between the trees. The trees were staked and an area around each tree maintained free of grass and weeds.

Extract from a history of the lime avenue at Stormont researched by Brian McNeill.[17]

Wartime felling in the Belfast area

The creation of the Stormont Estate was the only significant landscaping project in the Belfast area in the 1930s. In the following decade there was no encouragement to enhance the environment and there was a loss of woodland during the war. Forestry staff of the Ministry of Agriculture acted as agents for the Ministry of Supply which enforced compulsory felling of woods across Northern Ireland.[18] Around Belfast the most important woodland that was cut for timber during this period was in the lower part of Colin Glen in west Belfast.[19] A plantation around the crest of Collin Mountain may also have been cleared at this time.[20] However, there was only very limited felling at the well-wooded estates of Stormont and Stranmillis [21] and a plan by the Ministry of Agriculture to fell over 3,000 trees in the grounds of Belfast Castle in 1940 never took place.[22] It is possible that these woods were spared because these mansion houses and demesnes had been taken over by the military and the trees helped provide camouflage. Other urban sites that ended the war years with their woods intact included Belvoir Park, where ammunition dumps were hidden in the woods, and Malone, Wilmont and Ballydrain where military personnel were also based.

Belfast's street trees were not felled during the war, though a resident of Malone Park, a private road in south Belfast, recalled that they were told not to prune the avenue of limes as army vehicles were hidden here. The war years also affected other street trees when, despite the protests of the Corporation, the Ministry of Finance ordered the removal of metal tree guards in the search for scrap.[23]

THE NATIONAL TRUST
NORTHERN IRELAND COMMITTEE

PROFESSOR GREGG WILSON, O.B.E., M.A., PH.D., D.SC., M.R.I.A., *Chairman*
THE HON. THE EARL OF ANTRIM
A. E. BRETT
HIS HONOUR JUDGE T. J. CAMPBELL*
W. M. CAPPER, B. COM. SC.
D. A. CHART, D.LITT., I.S.O.
THE RT. HON. SAMUEL CUNNINGHAM
A. H. DAVISON
THE RT. HON. SIR THOMAS DIXON, BART., H.M.L.
A. S. G. LOXTON
J. M. MOGEY, M.A.
C. J. McKISACK
MAJOR J. R. PERCEVAL-MAXWELL, D.L., M.P.
MISS DOROTHY ROBERTSON
JOHN SEEDS, F.R.I.B.A.
R. S. ROGERS, *Hon. Secretary*
AUSTIN BROWN, *Hon. Treasurer*

Collin Glen Appeal Committee

PROFESSOR GREGG WILSON, O.B.E., M.A., PH.D., D.SC., M.R.I.A., *Chairman*
J. A. BARLOWE, B.A., J.P., *Belfast Co-operative Society Ltd.*
NELSON BELL, *Ulster Society for the Preservation of the Countryside*
G. H. BRYSON
PROFESSOR K. G. EMELEUS, M.A., PH.D., M.R.I.A.
WALTER GINN, *Holiday Fellowship*
SAM GIRVAN, *Youth Hostel Association of N. Ireland Ltd.*
JOSEPH P. GOSS
C. W. GRANT, O.B.E., LL.B., *Belfast Civic Society*
D. LINDSAY KEIR, M.A., LL.D.
J. W. S. LESTIR
C. J. McKISACK
D. M. G. NEWBURN, *Belfast County Scout Council*
MRS. ELEANOR GRAINGER, *Belfast Naturalists' Field Club*
J. H. TYLES, *Co-operative Holidays Association*
AUSTIN BROWN, *Hon. Treasurer*
R. S. ROGERS, *Hon. Secretary*

*We much regret the death of Judge Campbell which has occured since this appeal went to press.

Save Collin Glen

SAVE COLLIN GLEN

Collin Glen lies to the South West of Belfast about a mile from the city boundary. It is divided in two by the Glen Road where it curves round the foot of the hills.

The lower Glen has been destroyed. The upper Glen which lies immediately above the road between Black Hill and Colin Mountain is still intact, but it also is threatened.

There are 55 acres of woods in this lovely upper Glen. For generations people from Belfast and from Finaghy and Dunmurry have visited it and loved it. Children have played in it; Boy Scouts have learned their craft there; and families have picnicked on the grassy banks by the stream.

It has always been a place of beauty where many kinds of native Irish trees have sheltered a multitude of wild flowers, and is of such interest to geologists that as far back as 1860 the British Association sent a party to explore the bed of its stream.

Northern Ireland has already fewer trees proportionately than any other country in Europe except Iceland. Apparently present legislation does not enable the planning authorities to prevent the cutting of trees, and the Northern Ireland Committee of the National Trust therefore approached the owner, who was about to sell the trees as timber. He generously agreed to grant the Trust an option to buy them and the land on which they stand.

The National Trust which is a voluntary society with no Government grant has practically no funds in Northern Ireland which it could devote towards buying this property. It has however formed an appeal Committee, composed of persons interested in the preservation of the Glen and representatives of kindred associations. This Committee appeals to all people in Belfast and neighbourhood to contribute something, however small, to the fund.

We need £2,000. This will buy the upper Glen and will provide a small endowment fund for maintenance.

It is a good communal investment. Land vested in the National Trust cannot be sold or handed over to anyone else. The National Trust is bound by Act of Parliament to preserve the amenities and beauty of its holdings.

We believe the investment will pay a dividend. We believe that if the people of Belfast and Finaghy and Dunmurry subscribe to buy this place it will be an example of civic duty fulfilled, and that not only will future generations find health and pleasure there, but its acquisition may cause a growing awareness of civic responsibility.

We therefore ask you to give liberally and to give soon.

Signed on behalf of the Appeal Committee:

GREGG WILSON, Chairman.
R. S. ROGERS, Hon. Secretary.
AUSTIN BROWN, Hon. Treasurer.

Subscriptions should be sent to the Honorary Treasurer at 102 Donegall Street, Belfast, or to the Honorary Secretary at 29 Wellington Place, Belfast. Cheques should be made payable to "The National Trust, Collin Glen Fund."

To the Hon. Treasurer, National Trust,
Collin Glen Fund, 102 Donegall Street, Belfast.

I enclose cheque/P.O./cash to the value of_____ to be devoted entirely towards the purchase and preservation of Upper Collin Glen.

Name

Address

Promotion and protection of trees

Lobbying to protect the environment can be traced back to the formation of a local branch of the National Trust in 1936 and in the following year to the founding of the Ulster Society for the Preservation of the Countryside by Wilfrid Capper, a tireless campaigner for the environment. These organisations started to make an impact in the aftermath of the war, a time when there was enthusiasm for new approaches that would be for the betterment of all.

The first environmental campaign was in 1945 when the National Trust launched an appeal to save woodland in the upper part of Colin Glen, a site that had escaped wartime felling but remained under threat. The appeal was successful and around the same time the Trust started to raise funds to acquire another wood near Belfast, the beautiful mature beech trees at Minnowburn Beeches by the River Lagan.[24] The immediate post-war period also saw the formation of the Belfast Civic Society, which started environmental lobbying through a planning and amenities sub-committee. This raised awareness of many urban issues that are still relevant today, including the provision of bicycle parks, street cleaning, river pollution, creating small open spaces in the city and tree planting.[25]

In 1945 the first overall plan for the development of the city was published by the Planning Commission. It stressed the need to protect open spaces and included specific comments about trees. The report stated that, although the Belfast area was fortunate in being better wooded than much of Northern Ireland, it was of the utmost importance that trees should be preserved, and recommended the provision of additional powers to protect trees. It also argued for new parks and playgrounds in built-up areas and proposed that the growth of Belfast should be regulated. In particular the report stated that development should be restricted in the uplands around Belfast and in the Lagan Valley.[26]

The importance of policies to manage and develop the tree resource in Northern Ireland was again highlighted in *The Ulster Countryside*, a report published by the Planning Advisory Board in 1946. This made surprisingly wide-ranging and perceptive comments about trees. It advocated tree planting through the state forestry programme, by local authorities and by private landowners. Tree planting was proposed for all kinds of locations including increased state forestry on the most suitable rather than cheapest land and the planting of appropriate species of trees on small sites, waste spaces, in new housing estates and in farms and private gardens. Planting street trees was also encouraged; it was noted that this had become 'so neglected in Northern Ireland that such trees appear now as a strange novelty'. The report stressed the need for woodland management and advocated continuous selective thinning rather than clear felling. Like the 1945 planning proposals for Belfast, it called for legislation to protect trees and to enforce replanting where felling occurred. The report recognised the importance of increasing public interest in trees through involving school children in tree planting and providing trails, camp sites and other recreational opportunities in forests. A particularly interesting proposal was to develop a suitable woodland site (Tollymore Park in County Down was suggested) to promote tree culture.[27]

Unfortunately, the key recommendations in these planning reports were not implemented by government. The voluntary environmental sector however continued to develop through a partnership approach. This came about with the formation in 1954 of the Central Gardens Association, a federation of local gardening and horticultural societies.[28] Although its origins might suggest that the Association would have been of restricted interest, this was not the case. Community groups, foresters, parks managers and others working in government were involved and together helped to promote environmental awareness. The Central Gardens Association organised the Best Kept Village and Town competitions, encouraged the setting up of village improvement committees and published the annual *Ulster Garden Handbook*, with articles about parks, trees, plants and gardening. Around this time the Ulster Society for the Preservation of the Countryside organised environmental campaigns to encourage tree planting and tree protection. These included an 'Arbour Week' in 1951, tree planting to commemorate the Coronation in 1953 and an exhibition 'Trees in Towns' held at the George VI Youth Centre, Belfast in 1961.[29]

A new approach to looking at the environment was introduced by landscape architects. The first landscape architect to work in Northern Ireland was Robert Carson, who studied architecture in Sheffield, planning in Edinburgh and then moved to the University of Pennsylvania to study landscape

Minnowburn Beeches between Shaw's Bridge and Edenderry.

architecture. On his return to Northern Ireland in 1963 he set up a practice on the Malone Road and also lectured to engineers, architects and planners. He became a landscape consultant to the Northern Ireland Ministry of Development and in this role produced the first local publication on landscape aspects of road design, including tree planting by new roads and motorways.[30] The profession grew in Northern Ireland when, in 1964, landscape architects drawn from Britain, America and Europe came to Northern Ireland to work with architects and planners in the New City Design Team for the development of Craigavon.[31]

Cutting the grass at Woodvale Park in 1954.

The Northern Ireland government was slow to develop environmental legislation and it was only in 1965 that the Amenity Lands Act provided a basis for the protection of landscapes and for nature conservation. Two advisory committees, the Nature Reserves Committee and Ulster Countryside Committee, were set up at this time. The Amenity Lands Act was subsequently replaced by new wildlife and conservation legislation and in 1989 the Council for Nature Conservation and the Countryside took over the role of the advisory committees.[32]

One lasting outcome of the Ulster Countryside Committee was the formation of the Ulster Tree Committee which promoted 'Tree Week', the first event taking place from 13-18 November 1967. Forestry Division of the Ministry of Agriculture helped to ensure the success of Tree Week in its first year by distributing 36,000 trees. Every school, village and town was asked to organise the ceremonial planting of one tree, and farmers, families and organisations were also encouraged to take part.[33] Tree Week grew to become a popular annual event that soon spread throughout Ireland and to Britain.

Ulster Tree Week car sticker.

The Ministry of Agriculture in Northern Ireland provided advice and information on all aspects of horticulture, including tree planting, through a Horticultural Advisory Service. Staff produced leaflets, organised talks and held conferences on landscaping aimed at planners, landscape architects and other professionals.[34] The Ministry also had an important role in promoting trees through Forestry Division. Prior to 1955 the public had been excluded from all forests, but in this year forest recreation started to be developed with the opening of Tollymore Forest Park. In the 1960s visitors were further encouraged through 'Touring in the trees', a network of forest sites where caravans could be sited for short periods. Forestry Division also issued and enforced felling licences, which were introduced under the 1953 Forestry Act, though unfortunately the licensing system gradually fell into disuse.[35]

The poor state of planning in Northern Ireland was still apparent in the 1960s[36] and it was only at the end of this decade with the publication of the *Belfast Urban Area Plan* in 1969 that an attempt was made to develop a comprehensive plan for the city. Environmental recommendations included establishing linear parks that would provide access to the countryside, landscape wedges to retain the distinctiveness of communities, and the protection of the Lagan Valley and uplands around Belfast. The plan also advocated the employment of specialists to advise on landscaping aspects of planning and, like earlier documents, again highlighted the need for Tree Preservation Orders.[37]

The Wesley Tree, Lambeg. One of the first protected trees.

In the following decades planners gained ever-growing legislative responsibility for protecting the environment, ranging from planning requirements for individual developments to the designation of conservation areas and area plans. Planning Policy Statements that stress the importance of trees and landscapes have also been developed, including PPS2 (nature conservation), PPS6 (planning archaeology and the built heritage) and PPS7 (quality residential environments). Tree Preservation Orders (TPOs) were finally introduced into Northern Ireland legislation in 1973, administered through Planning Service. Initially, a start was made to protect trees of importance, such as the Wesley Tree, two intertwined beech trees associated with the founder of Methodism, growing at Chrome Hill, Lambeg. However, this proactive approach unfortunately did not last and TPOs have come to only be applied when trees are under immediate threat, by which time damage is often already done. In addition, there is insufficient monitoring of protected trees and enforcement is rare.[38]

The Northern Ireland Environment Agency (developed from Environment and Heritage Service in 2008) has responsibility for protecting areas of ecological importance and so far two woodland Areas of Special Scientific Interest have been declared in the Belfast region, at North Woodburn Glen (ash/hazel woodland) and Craigantlet (upland mixed ash wood). The value of some other woodlands near Belfast has been highlighted through listing as Local Nature Reserves, and several woods in the urban areas are presently proposed as Sites of Local Nature Conservation Importance (SLNCIs).[39]

Cherry blossom, Merville Garden Village in 2008.

Post-War tree planting

In the 1940s and 1950s there was no large-scale tree planting in Belfast. There was just one urban tree project of note, the planting of avenues of cherry trees in Merville Garden Village in Newtownabbey. The building of these distinctive flat-roofed terraces started in the late 1940s and the cherry trees are thought to have been planted around 1953-54. It was probably Edward Prentice Mawson, the consulting architect, who made the inspired decision to include these trees which in spring have an abundance of pink blossoms that create an exceptional scene against the white buildings and blue sky.[40]

The Corporation Parks Department had few staff and only a small budget in the post-war period. Even amongst the staff there was little concern about tree planting; it is recalled that although several parks had

Barnett Desmesne with its beautiful landscape of old parkland trees and grasslands is one of the key sites in the Lagan Valley. When this photograph of the main driveway was taken in the 1950s the land was still grazed by sheep, contained by metal fencing.

nurseries, they were not used for trees but for annual bedding and growing flowers to decorate places such as Belfast Castle and the City Hall.[41] In 1964 the need for more street tree planting was publicly acknowledged by the Director of Parks, but was not acted upon.[42] Although the Corporation acquired a number of sites around this time, including Barnett Demesne, the Waterworks, Glencairn, Belmont and the Wilmont Estate (Sir Thomas and Lady Dixon Park), it was recognised that there was no money to develop them.[43]

The only organisation planting significant numbers of trees in Northern Ireland during this period was Forestry Division of the Ministry of Agriculture. By the 1960s Forestry Division had started to become involved in some tree schemes in the Belfast area including planting clumps of coniferous and broadleaved trees along the first section of the M1 Motorway between Belfast and Lisburn, assisting the Housing Trust in greening some housing estates and developing a 10 year planting plan for the Stormont Estate.[44] Forestry Division also provided trees for planting on private land, including large numbers of small amenity sites that required as few as 100 trees.[45] At this time there was general support for the planting of conifers for amenity, and in some areas, such as the northern Lagan Valley, many small conifer plantations were created, generally of larch and Scots pine.[46] Experimentation with hybrid poplars led to forestry staff providing these trees for amenity planting, such as the white poplars planted in the early 1970s near Queen's University playing fields at the Upper Malone Road.[47] Another project that Forestry Division is thought to have been involved in was the planting of the alternating groups of poplars and alders along the banks of the River Lagan between Ormeau and Stranmillis.

The main work of Forestry Division involved planting and managing woods on land that they had direct responsibility for, including two important woods near Belfast, centred on the old demesnes of Belvoir Park and Purdysburn. At Belvoir, Forestry Division had initially been asked by the Housing Trust to plant two small blocks of woodland within the housing estate. Subsequent discussions resulted in the leasing of land to create a new urban wood towards the River Lagan. Planting, mainly of conifers, began in 1961 and this 'forest in a city' soon became a very popular amenity area with a network of woodland walks.[48] The old estate woods in Purdysburn Demesne had been unmanaged since the area was acquired for an asylum and, in an initial attempt to develop the site, the hospital authority felled and replanted four acres under a planting grant in 1955-56. Around this time, forestry staff were approached for advice about the management of the old woods and these discussions eventually resulted in part of the demesne being leased to Forestry Division. Areas of existing woodland were managed and some conifer blocks were planted, mainly with Norway spruce. Other important sites in the region where planting and woodland management have been undertaken include land in the vicinity of the Woodburn Reservoirs at Carrickfergus, sites by two reservoirs near Craigantlet in the Holywood hills and part of the Clandeboye Estate.[49]

From 1975, when Forestry Division became the Forest Service of the Department of Agriculture, the organisation was refocused and became less involved in the general promotion of trees. This was part of a wider review of central and local government and around this time the Horticultural Advisory Service came to an end, as did the Central Gardens Association and its publication the *Ulster Garden Handbook*. The New City Design Team that had worked at Craigavon was also disbanded, though this is recalled as having had a positive result of growing the profession of landscape architecture, as practitioners moved into planning or private practice. The new Department of the Environment became responsible for conservation, initially through a Conservation Division, subsequently expanded and developed to form the present Northern Ireland Environment Agency.[50]

This period of government reorganisation coincided with growing public awareness of conservation and the need to protect the environment. There was a move away from amenity planting schemes influenced by traditional forestry practice, and increased interest in broadleaved trees, and in particular in planting species best suited to particular habitats and of greatest value in supporting native wildlife. In addition, the need for urban regeneration and to enhance the landscape of the Belfast urban area had, by the 1970s, become a priority.

Belvoir Park, a working forest in the city.

8. The second great tree planting project

The impact on the landscape of the low level of tree planting and lack of woodland management during much of the 20th century had become apparent by the 1970s. Many woods in estates and parks had an uneven age structure, with predominantly mature trees, and concern was frequently expressed that when these eventually died there would be a lack of young and developing trees to replace them. The street tree population in Belfast was similarly dominated by old trees, and not only was there a need to plant new trees, but some of the existing trees had to be removed because they were in poor condition or because they had outgrown narrow pavement sites.

Environmental education began to be promoted in Britain, teachers' packs of environmental activities were appearing and environmental centres catering for school groups were opening. Throughout Britain people were being encouraged to get involved in the 'Plant a Tree in 73' campaign. Although this particular scheme was later to be criticised for the lack of aftercare of the saplings, many other highly successful environmental initiatives were subsequently launched.

Northern Ireland lagged behind Britain in promoting environmental issues, and the growing communal violence of 'the Troubles' made it difficult to generate interest in conservation. However, in an effort to improve the physical and social conditions in Belfast, government started to allocate large sums for environmental improvement and regeneration schemes. Government also funded community development, training and work experience programmes that provided opportunities for the voluntary sector to set up environmental projects in which people could enhance their neighbourhoods.

In the Belfast region there was a combination of increased funding, a focused approach by many sectors on environmental improvement and a widespread acceptance of the need to plant more trees and improve the urban landscape. This provided the impetus for what can be considered as the Second Great Tree Planting Project.

Planting in Belfast parks and open spaces

Following government reorganisation in 1973 parks became one of the more important departments within the new Belfast City Council. A larger budget was allocated and there were major developments such as the rebuilding of the zoo and the refurbishment of Belfast Castle. Attention then turned to tree planting on an impressive scale at both recently-acquired sites and the older parks.

Initially, trees were bought in (mainly from Holland and England) and kept at nursery yards in parks including Belfast Castle, Ormeau and at the City Cemetery until they were needed. In the mid-1970s Belfast City Council acquired 100 acres of farmland at Beechvale, near La Mon Hotel in Castlereagh,

Children from Hollybank Primary School at Monkstown Wood, Newtownabbey,
taking part in the Woodland Trust 'Trees for All' Campaign in 2006.

93

where a centralised nursery was set up with around 16 members of staff looking after trees and other plant material. In the first year of operation 2,000 standard trees (around 2m high) were purchased and grown on in the nursery for planting in parks. Subsequently, the nursery was annually stocked with about 600-700 standards and 20,000 whips (young single-stem trees).[1]

When large-scale planting started in parks there were very high levels of vandalism. For example, at Alexandra Park in 1982 it was reported that over half of the 3,610 trees planted had died or been vandalised. A memo sent to Craig Wallace, Director of Parks, noted that at Glencairn 'there is ample room for planting to the rear of Fernhill House but unfortunately every single one planted last year was destroyed. I have to ask, is it worth it?'[2] However, despite setbacks, increased funding allowed staff to continue to undertake large-scale environmental schemes, and overall losses accounted for only a small percentage of the trees planted, as described by the Director of Parks in 1985:

> We find that if you do things on a small scale nobody thanks you. They make no impact. If you plant in twenties and hundreds the vandals can destroy most of them. But if you plant in thousands and tens of thousands the vandals can make less impact. We have to think big. That is our philosophy. Do things on a generous enough scale and people can't help but notice.[3]

To counter the problem of vandalism, a variety of ideas were tried. Sometimes a high percentage of alder and willow was included as these species grow quickly and come again if vandalised. At a number of places prickly plants such as hawthorn and vigorous ornamental roses were included in the planting mix to deter vandals. Some park managers also tried to protect new clumps of trees in parks by including an outer ring of hawthorn.

The size of trees planted also changed in response to vandalism. Initially planting was mainly of large trees as this gave an instant effect, though it was found that these conspicuous trees were more often destroyed than areas planted with small trees. Increasingly, planting in open ground in parks was of closely spaced whips.[4] The emphasis on planting small trees was reinforced when in 1987 parks superintendents were asked to attend in-house lectures on 'Tree whip planting – the Department's Policy.' In the following year there was further encouragement to plant trees when the new Head of Parks asked managers to draw up five-year planting plans for all open spaces. These were subject to regular review and the Head of Parks frequently undertook site visits to check on progress.[5]

The impact of large-scale tree planting was perhaps most noticeable at Victoria and Ormeau Parks, two sites that were transformed from mainly mown grass with spaced mature trees into predominantly woodland. At some locations, including Falls Park and Belmont Park, avenues were planted to great effect. Trees were planted around the boundaries of many parks. Tree planting also transformed playing fields. Traditionally, the only trees by pitches had been rows of fast growing tall, upright poplars to act as windbreaks. This policy was revised in the 1980s when land surrounding playing fields was planted with mixtures of mainly broadleaved native trees. When ownership of several playing fields around Belfast was transferred to Belfast Parks from the Department of Education in 1987, land around these pitches was also planted.[6]

The scale of planting was impressive. For example at Victoria Park 23,000 whips were planted in 1989. In 1990 at Tommy Patton Memorial Park 11,000 young trees were planted and during the following year a mechanical digger was used to excavate holes in hardcore to provide space for 800 standard trees. In south Belfast, 570 whips were listed for planting in Lyric Wood in 1989-1990, and around this time 1,200 trees were planted at Annadale. In north Belfast at Carr's Glen 13,000 whips and 290 standard trees were planted in 1982 and it is recalled that around 10,000 trees were planted in the grounds of Belfast Castle. Around two acres of new woodland were created at Ligoniel Park and at Glenbank Park 1,600 whips of native species were planted. This scale of planting was replicated at most other parks.[7] A few new parks were also developed and planted during the 1980s including Cathedral Gardens, a former car park by Saint Anne's Cathedral that was landscaped with trees, shrubs, seating and a water feature, and Knocknagoney and Forth River linear parks. In many places woodland creation was accompanied by the planting of drifts of daffodil bulbs and in 1983 interpark competitions were launched to support improvements including the best spring and summer displays of colour.[8]

In some parks tree planting was undertaken as part of wider environmental improvement schemes. For example, in the late 1980s a wooded island was created in the upper lake at the Waterworks to enhance the landscape and to provide wildlife habitat. Brick rubble was used to form the island, which was planted with trees, willow pegs and clumps of reed. Around the lake standard trees were planted and patches of woodland were developed mainly with alder, white willow, birch, poplar and ash and with some tall-growing trees like beech, oak and Scots pine.[9]

Experimental planting was undertaken on the Council tip site at Duncrue to provide screening along the M2 Motorway and Dargan Road, and to see if woodland could be established in these very poor ground conditions. This project started in 1980 and continued for the next 8 years with thousands of whips of native species, mainly alder, willow and poplar, planted into a layer of subsoil spread over the compacted rubbish. No fertiliser was used and there was no aftercare, other than thinning the plantations. The scheme was considered to be very successful and indicated that once the landfill site was closed and capped the area could be effectively landscaped.[10]

Tree planting in parks declined during the 1990s, though in recent years this has to some extent been addressed through restructuring resulting in the appointment of managers based in parks allowing them to develop a more 'hands on' approach to developing their sites. Another positive development has been a reduction in the level of vandalism of trees in parks, to the extent that this is no longer a significant issue. The appointment of biodiversity officers within local authorities is increasingly acting as a stimulus for woodland management including thinning, controlling invasive species and the development of ground flora. In Belfast parks surveys have also highlighted the need to prevent woodlands from encroaching important habitats such as the species-rich meadows at Barnett Demense and Sir Thomas and Lady Dixon Park.

Street tree programme

In 1973 responsibility for roads passed from local authorities to the Roads Executive (soon renamed Roads Service) and agreement was reached with Belfast Parks to plant and manage street trees using tree squads. A small street planting programme was initiated and included fastigiate hornbeam, an attractively shaped tree with upwards growing branches not previously seen on Belfast's streets. In 1979 Belfast City Council employed its first tree specialist (arboriculturalist), Fiona Holdsworth, and one of her tasks was to draw up plans for an expanded street tree planting and tree maintenance programme. Initially concerns were raised about street trees shading road lighting, leaves blocking gullies and roots damaging underground services. However, as planting got underway it became accepted that there were few problems and that these were far outweighed by the value of trees in enhancing the city.[11]

In 1983 a deputation from Belfast City Council met with Chris Patten, Under Secretary of State, to highlight the lack of funding for street tree planting and tree care. This resulted in financial support from the recently-formed Belfast Development Office of the Department of the Environment for parks staff to plant 400

Fastigiate hornbeam in autumn. Lancefield Road, off the Lisburn Road.

street trees.[12] A tree survey undertaken at this time identified 5,491 street trees in Belfast, mostly mature lime or plane,[13] and a maintenance programme was developed with details of each street tree held on a computer database. Another advance was the introduction of modern tree climbing techniques which enabled trees to be pruned while ensuring that the shape of the tree was retained.

A wider range of street trees were planted, predominantly small-growing species best suited to congested city streets. Diversifying the street tree population also added interest and reduced the risk of the spread of pests and diseases. The main species planted at this time were small-leaved lime, maple, fastigiate hornbeam, ash, cherry, rowan and whitebeam. Ornamental pear (*Pyrus calleryana* 'Chanticleer') was increasingly used as it has an attractive shape and is in leaf for much of the year. Cherry and rowan trees were subsequently avoided as the shallow roots of cherry cause pavement damage and rowan was found to die off in dry weather. In the earlier plantings select standard trees were used though it was found that larger extra-heavy standard trees protected by a temporary mesh guard fixed to the tree stake suffered less from vandalism. More recently there has been a trend to plant root-staked semi-mature trees to create an even greater instant impact, in some schemes protected by permanent ornamental steel guards.[14]

Priority has been given to planting trees along arterial routes (including the Lisburn, Ormeau, Crumlin, Antrim and Shore Roads) and streets in the city centre,[15] though wherever roads are resurfaced and tree pits can be dug as part of a road contract, consideration is given to planting trees. Interplanting is undertaken to fill gaps and create a mixed-age population, for example along Annadale Embankment. A street tree sponsorship scheme has been developed and well-known personalities have been asked to plant pavement trees to create a Celebrity Tree Trail. The Belfast Parks street tree programme has continued to develop and by 2008 was responsible for managing an impressive 15,000 street trees throughout greater Belfast and in Lisburn, north Down, Ards, Newtownabbey and also in Ballymena.[16]

Planting in housing estates

In the 1950s and 1960s the Housing Trust (now the Northern Ireland Housing Executive) acquired large areas of land around Belfast for public housing. Some of these housing estates, including Belvoir Park, Rathfern and Seymour Hill, were former demesnes and included areas of mixed broadleaved woodland, parkland and some long-established native woodland. Tall exotic trees like giant redwood (Wellingtonia) and

Housing and tower blocks in old estate woodland at Dunmurry.

Monterey cypress were also often present. To provide space for new housing some trees were inevitably felled, but it was recognised that it was important to retain areas of grassland, woodland and the more scenic areas such as river valleys for amenity and recreation. This resulted in the preservation of individual specimen trees and mature woods near residential estates. For example, at Belvoir Park the wooded valleys and parkland towards the River Lagan were kept as open space, and housing development was restricted to the south eastern part of the demesne. At Rathfern houses were built on the lower ground, and old estate woodland on the slopes of Carnmoney Hill was left as an informal playground for children and a haven for wildlife. At Seymour Hill housing was excluded from the attractive landscapes near the River Lagan and Derriaghy Glen.[17]

Initially there was only a small amount of tree planting in housing estates, undertaken on 'supply and plant' contracts, and areas of grassland were largely kept as regularly mown lawns with shrub beds. There was some planting of large, expensive semi-mature trees to provide instant impact. Planting plans were developed for some estates - for example the landscape architect Robert Carson drew up early schemes for housing estates in Castlereagh.[18]

In the 1970s a concerted effort was made to 'green' housing estates. This was done to improve the quality of the environment and tree planting was also seen as a good way of employing the grass-cutting crews in the winter months. In 1973 a Landscape Group was set up by the Executive to design the grounds of housing schemes, and within a year the Housing Executive opened Millmount Farm Nursery at Comber Road, Dundonald. This was the main nursery for the Executive and was run by over 20 staff.

The nursery functioned largely as a holding centre but trees and plants were also grown on in fields. Every year thousands of standard and extra-heavy trees, as well as smaller trees, whips and shrubs, were bought in, mainly from Holland. These went out for planting in housing estates in trailer-loads every day during the planting season. Maintenance of the plantings was the responsibility of regional grounds supervisors. However, there were difficulties with the operation of the nursery and, with the introduction of Compulsory Competitive Tendering, the system for planting trees was re-evaluated. It was found to be cheaper to put the supply of trees and shrubs out to contract rather than to run the Millmount Nursery, which shut in the 1980s. Despite these changes, the rate of tree planting did not decline and indeed is recalled as having continued to expand until the late 1980s and early 1990s.[19]

Planting schemes in housing estates have frequently combined barrier planting, amenity planting and garden trees. Whips have generally been used for the barrier planting, with willow and alder as a nurse crop, and tall-growing species like oak and beech that will, in time, become dominant. In large areas of mown grassland, tall standard or extra-heavy standard staked trees with temporary wire cages are often dotted around as amenity planting. Generally colourful trees have been chosen, including Norway maple, Swedish whitebeam, cherry and birch. In some estates large rootballed conifers have been tried, though these have generally not taken well. Unfortunately, staked trees planted in grassland areas often suffer damage from strimmers and lawnmowers and the level of vandalism of these trees has been high.[20]

In more urban areas, streets of old terraced housing that had lacked gardens or any green space have been replaced by lower density Housing Executive developments. These have where possible incorporated small gardens, street trees and raised brick planters in shared surface areas. There has often been community consultation about these projects; for example in 1977 when Roden Street was being redeveloped, 60 young people from the area were given a conducted tour of Millmount Farm Nursery and shown the trees and plants that were to be used. Landscape architects explained how this new greenery would enhance their streets, and the children were encouraged to keep an eye on the new plantings.[21]

Trees continue to be planted in Belfast housing estates, though with the decline in house building by the Housing Executive, and the majority of the houses in estates now being owner-occupied, the activities of the Executive, including tree planting, have decreased.

Housing Executive development off Dublin Road.

Tree planting and urban regeneration

In 1971 a start was made to improve the urban environment though the 'Brighter Belfast Campaign' organised by the Community Relations Commission which, with help from the Corporation's Technical Services Department, tidied up sites around the city. This was followed by the central government funded 'Cosmetic Campaign Scheme' which provided 100% grants for environmental projects to enhance Belfast. The aim was to provide instant impact, and Belfast Parks undertook much of the work including the first large-scale planting of flowers to brighten the city centre. This commenced in May 1973 with the placing of 300 containers filled with 750 dozen bedding plants on city streets.[22] The Cosmetic Campaign Scheme was in turn replaced by another wonderfully named project, the 'Spruce-up Scheme', which was managed by the Department of the Environment, again with 100% project funding. This was initially targeted at sites affected by civil disturbances and areas of social deprivation, though by 1978 it had a broad objective of encouraging environmental improvement throughout Northern Ireland.[23]

One of the earlier large urban regeneration projects was the pedestrianisation of parts of the city centre around Ann Street and Cornmarket, work that included the planting of trees and shrubs in large raised brick planters on these paved streets. The planters were found to provide a reasonable environment for tree growth, though all too often they attracted vandals and acted as receptacles for rubbish. Another project from the early 1970s involved the removal of the disused railway embankment from Dee Street to the Holywood Arches to create the Ballymacarrett Walkway, a strip of open space in the heavily built-up inner east of the city.[24]

By 1981 around one million pounds a year was being spent on physical regeneration projects in Belfast and the impetus for environmental improvement continued to grow with the formation by government of the Belfast Development Office, Belfast Regeneration Office and Making Belfast Work. Belfast City Council set up a landscape planning and development team within the parks section and these staff became involved in projects throughout Belfast. Another statutory organisation that contributed to urban landscaping was Roads Service, which undertook planting along the main routes into the city, including the Westlink, which was landscaped with mainly native species of trees underplanted with ivy and daffodil bulbs.[25]

Publicity shot for tree planting at Fountain Street in the city centre in April 1997.

Some environmental improvement projects were designed to be short-term measures to mask urban dereliction, in the knowledge that the sites would be subsequently redeveloped. This approach was used at May's Meadow, where about 10 years after this vacant site was improved by landscaping and planting, the land was cleared and used for a mixed business and residential development. Other urban regeneration schemes were primarily nature conservation projects, such as the wading bird habitat developed at the Kinnegar lagoon near the city airport and the enhancement of the Bog Meadows wet meadow habitat in south Belfast. The government-funded nature walk created by Conservation Volunteers along the old Comber railway line in Bloomfield was designed to encourage wildlife as well as forming an attractive walkway on what had been an unsightly dumping ground.[26]

The riverside area in Belfast had a number of derelict sites including the disused gasworks, the former cattle pens and fish market at Oxford Street and unsightly scrap metal yards along Queen's Quay. This land was recognised as having great potential for a mixed development that would revitalise Belfast and refocus the city along the Lagan and docklands. It was designated Laganside and a Concept Plan published in 1987 was implemented by the new Laganside Corporation. Significant new areas of green space were proposed, with tree and shrub planting along riverside walks and new public squares by the Custom House and as part of the Waterfront Hall development. A main focus for Laganside was improving the appearance of the River Lagan in the urban area and enhancing water quality. A new weir was constructed at the mouth of the river and a system to aerate and mix the estuarine water by pumping air through underwater pipes was installed.[27] Wildlife was attracted to the area by the creation of a gently sloping gravel river bank from the Blackstaff to Maysfield, where trial planting with clumps of reeds brought from Stranmillis demonstrated that this brackish water habitat would develop into a wildlife resource. However proposals for a wildlife island, willow and alder planting on riverbanks and perching posts for cormorants unfortunately did not proceed.[28]

New city parks and public spaces were created through urban regeneration schemes, mostly in the 1980s and 1990s. One such example was the development of a new park by clearing away buildings in front of Saint Anne's Cathedral. At the Crescent, between Botanic Avenue and University Road, an area of unmanaged grass was developed into an attractive public space. In keeping with the surrounding Victorian buildings, which form part of a building conservation area, this was designed as a traditional park with ornate metal railings and a circular walk lined with tall false acacia trees, a species not often planted in Belfast. A smaller public space was created in the late 1980s at Amelia Street, behind the Crown Bar, where semi-mature lime and birch trees were planted on a paved surface. Probably the biggest trees planted were five fully grown lime and birch brought to Belfast in the 1989-1990 planting season to form an instant urban green space on the wide pavement at Castle Place in the centre of Belfast. Although trees of this size are difficult to transplant, they showed no sign of stress and grew well.[29]

An innovative project involved the planting of the eastern approaches to the new cross harbour road bridge. Here it was decided to plant trees directly into embankments formed only of crushed slate and shale. Research into the properties of this material (known locally as 'grizzly') and the difficulties of using it as a growing medium for trees was undertaken by the University of Ulster. Planting took place in 1995, the year the road opened, and has been successful. Plants that can fix nitrogen, like Italian alder and false acacia, have grown well. In addition, plants suited to nutrient-poor conditions, like sea buckthorn and buddleia, are thriving and a range of other species, including hawthorn, hazel, willows and burnet rose have survived. Fertiliser has not been used as this would have encouraged weed growth which would have competed with the saplings.[30]

By the late 1990s the improvement in community relations, growth in the economy and reduction in unemployment, coupled with greater private sector investment in Belfast, allowed a reduction in government funding for urban regeneration projects. However, new schemes are still being developed.

Creating community woodlands

The pioneering work of the Ulster Society for the Protection of the Countryside and the National Trust, together with schemes like Tree Week and the Best Kept Village competition, had started to focus public interest on protecting and enhancing the environment. The role of the voluntary environmental movement developed further with the formation of a local office of the Royal Society for the Protection of Birds in

1966 and the founding of the Ulster Trust for Nature Conservation (now Ulster Wildlife Trust) in 1978. These charities developed educational programmes, lobbied on conservation issues and acquired land for nature reserves. Practical conservation started to be undertaken by a local group called Grassroots and this role quickly developed with the formation of Conservation Volunteers Northern Ireland in 1983. These groups decided to use only native species of trees in amenity schemes, an idea that is now accepted practice in the conservation movement but at the time was considered radical.[31]

This period of increased activity by voluntary organisations coincided with the worst of the Troubles in Northern Ireland. At times of heightened tension street trees were often vandalised or felled with chainsaws to act as barricades. Some became impregnated with shrapnel from bomb blasts. In 1973, when the Middle Falls Environmental and Community Development Committee wrote to the Director of Parks to ask for street tree planting and the replacement of trees on the Falls Road that had been destroyed, the request had to be refused. The Director of Parks wrote in his reply that 'you will appreciate that at the present time there is a very real and added difficulty in persuading work squads to go into certain areas of the city. We can only hope that the situation will improve.'[32] Across Northern Ireland huge bonfires were annually built by both communities and in the search for anything flammable many trees in parks and housing estates were cut down, a scene reported by one journalist in 1977.

> *July and August are a conservationist's nightmare – all those kids running around with hatchets cutting down anything that's growing. Last week in Derry I saw gangs of them dragging the remains of a butchered sycamore into a local housing estate. The next day I saw the same spectacle in Belfast on the North Circular Road – a couple of teenagers dragging a semi-mature tree towards Ballysillan.*[33]

Throughout Northern Ireland, and particularly in Belfast, the deteriorating political and economic situation led to an urgent need to create employment and involve people in ways that would make a positive contribution to the community. One of the early responses by government was an employment relief scheme called the Urban and Rural Improvement Campaign. This was supported by Forestry Division, which by the mid 1970s had around 1,000 people in schemes to create public facilities in forests throughout Northern Ireland, work that included enhancing the old arboretum at Belvoir Forest Park.[34] Another organisation developed by government at this time was Enterprise Ulster, which, particularly in

Celebrating the planting by Conservation Volunteers of half a million trees, Crawfordsburn Country Park, 1991.

its early days, undertook amenity projects. One such example from 1973 involved 25 men who were given the task of improving public access to Cave Hill by cutting back vegetation and laying paths.[35]

The Action for Community Employment (ACE) scheme was set up in the early 1980s and generally operated through partnerships between government and the voluntary sector. The scheme was focused on long-term unemployed people who could apply for a one-year job in an organisation with charitable aims to gain training and work experience by doing tasks that would benefit the community. Environmental charities rapidly expanded by setting up teams of ACE workers and employing them in roles that included administration, promotion and education work, as well as practical conservation tasks. In addition to the established environmental organisations, local community associations were created to utilise ACE staff to plant trees, undertake gardening for the elderly, create community gardens, tidy housing estates and do other amenity work. Many groups ran an ACE scheme of 40 staff, to qualify for two full-time management 'core posts'.[36] Volunteering programmes were set up by some environmental charities including Conservation Volunteers, which developed an impressive range of training courses to help participants gain skills and accredited qualifications in practical conservation and land management.

The range of voluntary organisations focused on environmental work in the Belfast area grew through the 1990s to include Bryson House, Colin Glen Trust, Conservation Volunteers, Forest of Belfast, Grassroots, Groundwork, International Tree Foundation, National Trust, NI2000, RSPB, Voluntary Service Belfast, Voluntary Service Lisburn, Ulster Wildlife Trust and, by the end of the decade, also the Woodland Trust. In addition, local pressure groups such as the Save Belvoir Park and Save Hydebank Wood campaigns made an impact in raising awareness of sites that were under threat.

The rapid growth in the number of statutory and voluntary organisations undertaking tree projects prompted the inclusion of a policy on urban forestry in the *Belfast Urban Area Plan 2001* (published in 1990).[37] This policy 'to make trees an integral part of the urban fabric' led to the formation of the Forest of Belfast urban forestry partnership to support a more strategic approach to tree planting and tree care throughout the urban area. One of its early tasks was a comprehensive survey of trees throughout Greater Belfast. Events to involve all of the main environmental organisations were initiated, including Tree Fairs at Belvoir Park Forest in 1993 and 1996 which attracted thousands of visitors. Encouragement has been given to partner organisations to plant more trees, and local groups in Greater Belfast have been

Measuring giant redwood trees (Wellingtonia) at Hunterhouse School.

directly aided through the 'Trees for the Community' project in which 120,000 free trees were distributed from 1997 to 2000. The Forest of Belfast has been particularly active in promoting tree care, including encouraging the monitoring and enforcement of Tree Preservation Orders. In 2002, a booklet *Trees and Development* was produced jointly with Planning Service, the Landscape Architects Branch of Construction Service and the Construction Employers Federation. The Forest of Belfast has also developed innovative ways of increasing awareness of trees through a volunteer Tree Warden scheme, implementing Belfast's first environmental arts initiative 'Art in the Park' and exploring and celebrating the historical and cultural importance of trees.[38]

The estimated tree population for Greater Belfast is 732,340 trees.

Short lived, smaller species of trees such as alder and willow are most frequently found in Greater Belfast, though evergreen conifers and cherry trees are most common in gardens.

The greatest diversity of trees occurs in Lisburn and Newtownabbey, the lowest diversity in the more rural Edenderry area.

Overall, nearly 60% of the trees are in public areas such as parks, along roads and around housing estates, though this figure varies throughout the region; in central Belfast nearly all the trees are in public ownership, whereas the reverse in true in Edenderry.

Central Belfast, Edenderry, Lisburn and Newtownabbey have the lowest density of trees (less than 40 trees/ha). Castlereagh, west Belfast and Holywood have slightly higher density of trees (40-50 trees/ha) and south, north and east Belfast have the highest density of trees (60-90 trees/ha). The average tree density in Belfast is 46 trees/ha.

19.7% of trees surveyed were under 3 years old, 57.5% immature, 22.8% mature. Holywood has the highest percentage of mature trees (c. 50%).

Tree condition in Belfast is generally good, with almost 70% of trees in sound condition, though in some areas the figure is less than 50%.

Key findings of a survey undertaken in 1993 and 1994 of over 36,000 trees by the Forest of Belfast Initiative.[39]

Environmental education programmes were developed in the Belfast area from the early 1980s, starting with the appointment of Dr Robert Scott as education officer for Belfast City Council Parks Department. A Nature Study Centre that included a crawl-through badger sett for children was opened at Sir Thomas and Lady Dixon Park and a popular annual 'Tree Teach-in' organised for children.[40] In 1982 Forest Service opened an Education Room and created displays in the courtyard buildings at Belvoir Park Forest. An education officer was based at Belvoir and part-time guides were employed to deliver their 'Forest Classroom' programme. Environment and Heritage Service (now Northern Ireland Environment Agency) developed a visitor centre at Crawfordsburn Country Park in 1988. The larger environmental charities have also employed education officers to run programmes at sites they manage and outreach programmes at schools, where practical work such as tree planting, pond creation and wildlife gardening can be undertaken.[41] Although environmental education programmes cover all the main habitats, woodlands are often a focus: they have a diverse flora and fauna (leaf litter hunts for mini-beasts are forever popular), are safe for children, and are generally robust environments undamaged by large numbers of visitors.

Voluntary organisations have made an important contribution to developing and managing sites in the Belfast area. These have included urban nature reserves, parks, green corridors with footpaths and small open spaces. The first charity to become active in this role was Bryson House, which in the 1980s set up community gardens in Belfast. Conservation Volunteers took on a number of major site-based projects in the urban area. One of the most impressive was the Beersbridge Nature Walk, where paths, ponds, woodland and wildflower meadows were laid out along a disused railway line during the period 1985-1995. The Laurel Glen project has operated throughout Poleglass since 1988 and has involved tree and wildflower planting, path building, rubbish clearing and pond creation. Other long-term urban projects have included work at Cherryvalley, Tillysburn and TRACS, The Railways Amenity and Conservation Scheme, which expanded an earlier project to plant trees on urban railway embankments, cuttings and stations. Conservation Volunteers also set up a hugely successful tree nursery at Clandeboye, which has developed to become the main supplier of trees for environmental projects throughout the region and is used by many residents to provide trees for gardens and farms. Most of the trees in the nursery are grown from local seed and this charity has played a lead role in the promotion of local provenance seed sources through its Seeds of Time and Place project.[42]

The most important woodland site developed through community action has been Colin Glen, a narrow river valley that stretches from the Stewartstown Road up into the Belfast Hills. The glen had deteriorated since its heyday as a wooded Victorian estate; trees had been felled during the war, brickworks pits had been excavated and there had been extensive dumping. Local people became interested in trying to improve the glen and in the mid-1980s the Department of the Environment undertook to cap an unsightly dump on the site. The Colin Glen Trust was formed in 1989 with local representatives of both communities to develop the valley by actively managing the site and encouraging access. An education programme, volunteering scheme and a ranger service have been developed and the former British Legion hall on the Stewartstown Road transformed into an attractive park centre. A unique and innovative aspect of the work of the Colin Glen Trust has been the development of a golf course and driving range at the lower end of the glen. This has preserved open space, linked recreation with conservation and provided new opportunities to engage with local residents. Income from the golf course has been used to support the conservation work of the Trust.[43]

Government support for community environmental projects has been provided mainly by the Northern Ireland Environment Agency and through urban regeneration funding. The Forest Service's Community Woodland Supplement to the Woodland Grant Scheme has also encouraged private landowners and councils to create public woodlands. In Belfast parks the public have been involved in creating woodlands through tree sponsorship schemes. These is a Commemorative Tree Scheme at Roselawn Cemetery, a community arboretum at Barnett Demesne, and at Belfast Castle Estate a 'Family Tree Site' has been developed in partnership with the Forest of Belfast Initiative and the International Tree Foundation.[44]

The voluntary environmental sector has had difficulty in developing further because of the limitations of funding, which is often in the form of three-year 'start-stop' grants. The running down and eventual closure of the ACE scheme in the late 1990s was understandable, given the improving economy and high levels of employment, though this had a major impact on community development and the work of many small charities. However, the energy and commitment that characterises the voluntary movement ensures the continued development of campaigns to enhance the environment. This can be seen from examples of millennium tree projects. Conservation Volunteers Millennium Tree Campaign involved 80,000 people in the planting of one and a half million trees from 1997-2001. The Yew Trees for the New Millennium scheme set up by the Forest of Belfast distributed yews, trees that can live for a thousand years, for planting in churchyards and graveyards of all denominations around Belfast. It also organised the Lord

Stork with Council hat used to promote the Lord Mayor's Millenium Baby Tree Scheme.

Mayor's Millennium Baby Tree Scheme in partnership with Belfast City Council, which provided a garden tree for the parents of Belfast babies born in the millennium year. By far the largest millennium tree project was the UK-wide Woods on your Doorstep campaign of the Woodland Trust. As part of this project the Trust developed 51 new woods with public access across Northern Ireland, most on Housing Executive land and with support from Forest Service grants. In the Belfast region an impressive range of sites was taken into the scheme. Residents can now go for a walk in Woods on your Doorstep at Throne and Ligoniel in north Belfast, the Woodland Walkway at Clara Park in east Belfast and the Friends of Belvoir Wood in Castlereagh. In Newtownabbey extensive woods were developed at Rathfern and Monkstown, and around Lisburn woods were created at Seymour Hill and Old Warren.[45]

Planting acorns from Belvior in a seed bed at the Conservation Volunteers tree nursery.

Innovative projects to improve the environment have continued post-millennium. One such example is the Green Gym scheme of Conservation Volunteers, which began when a group of people at a Belfast day care centre were encouraged to undertake practical conservation work. Green Gym partnerships now include the Mater Hospital Occupational Therapy Department, Knockbracken Healthcare Trust, schools, women's groups and businesses. With appropriate support and training, the scheme helps people to improve their health and sense of wellbeing through exercise and undertaking environmental improvement projects. Other new environmental projects are being developed through a five-year Lagan Valley Regional Park partnership, launched in 2008 with support from the Heritage Lottery Fund. These projects will include volunteers collecting thousands of acorns from the ancient oaks at Belvoir, our oldest dated wood, for planting throughout the Lagan Valley.[46]

Environmental art. One of the oak figures by the Malone Road commissioned by the Forest of Belfast to promote city trees.

9. The future of the urban forest

Belfast is fortunate to have some very old woodlands and a fascinating heritage of trees planted and nurtured in estates, parks, gardens, and in streets. Thanks to an impressive level of planting in recent decades by a wide range of organisations the age structure of our tree population is improving. However, is all well in the urban forest?

First, let's look at the young plantations. Despite campaigns to stress the importance of a few minutes' aftercare to ensure the development of young trees, sadly it is still commonplace to find saplings swamped by weeds. In amenity areas trees are all too often skinned by the careless use of strimmers and lawnmowers. In young woods the need for thinning is all too often forgotten. Where trees are planted by contractors at development sites like supermarket car parks there is rarely any maintenance and staked trees are 'strangled', damaged and sometimes slowly killed because tree ties are not loosened.

TREE CARE WEEK
25 - 31 JULY 1998

SKINNED BY STRIMMERS

CHOKED BY WEEDS

STRANGLED BY A FORGOTTEN TREE TIE

CHECK YOUR TREES IN TREE CARE WEEK

Produced by The Forest of Belfast Initiative, a partnership of organisations promoting urban tree planting & care. For further information ☎ 01232 - 270350

Going, going, gone. The death of an oak tree in Newtownabbey because of trenching. This tree had been protected by a Tree Preservation Order but a year after the trench had been dug it was almost leafless. It was subsequently removed.

Going from the youngest trees to the oldest, does the evidence on the ground show that we are protecting our best mature trees? The answer, unfortunately, has to be no. In Greater Belfast increasing intensification of housing (sometimes called 'urban cramming') is causing the loss of many old gardens and their mature specimen trees. It is heartening to note that Planning Service is placing Tree Preservation Orders on an increasing number of trees, and all trees in building conservation areas are now protected. However, it is a depressing fact that at development sites trees to be retained are frequently damaged during building work. This is most commonly because, contrary to planning conditions, protective fencing is not erected at the outer spread of the branches prior to the start of development work to create a 'protection zone' of undisturbed land which should be maintained until the work is completed. This is essential to ensure that tree roots are not cut by trenching nor damaged by the movement of heavy vehicles and the dumping of materials under the trees. There is an urgent need for monitoring and enforcement that is effective and protects the best of our natural environment. Given the low level of tree cover in Northern Ireland it is also difficult to understand why this is the only part the British Isles where there is currently no system of felling licences.

There is some hope for our tree heritage. The Woodland Trust has recently completed a study using old maps and field evidence to identify long-established woods in Northern Ireland and their Ancient Tree Hunt should build on work by the Tree Council of Ireland and others to identify our 'champion trees'. However, pin-pointing old woods and veteran trees is still only a first step. There is a growing need to ensure that the best of our trees and woods are fully protected and are actively managed. The prime example of a wood under threat is Belvoir Park. This wooded former demesne, which has an impressive number of veteran oaks, is of regional importance and yet there is currently a plan for a bus route to be constructed amongst the trees.

Our old trees and woods are also under threat from climate change, diseases and pests. Although woods can appear timeless, the spread of Dutch elm disease and the arrival of the grey squirrel in our urban woods serve as reminders of just how fragile they are.

The disappearance of elm, a tree that rivalled oak for size and grandeur, has made a dramatic change to our woods. The devastating effects of Dutch elm disease were first seen in the Belfast area in the 1980s, at Barnett Demesne. Attempts were made to treat specimen elms by pumping fungicide into the trunk of trees though this was expensive, time consuming and ultimately proved to be unsuccessful. Another approach that was tried involved instigating a sanitation policy: infected trees were identified and felled and the bark was removed before trunks were moved. However, not all large landowners managed the disease and it quickly spread. Almost without our noticing, one by one the big old trees died. Today nearly all the elms we see are saplings, suckers from the rootstock of old elms which when they develop into more substantial trees become infected.[1] The appearance of pest species is also of great concern. The most obvious example is the grey squirrel, deliberately introduced into County Longford around 100 years ago. They spread slowly at first, but by the early 1950s they were spotted in County Armagh and in recent years greys appeared in Belfast woods including Cave Hill and Carnmoney Hill and at the Foster Green Hospital at the top of the Ormeau Road. At sites like Barnett Demesne where reds were present greys soon became dominant. By 2004 greys were seen in some suburbs of the city and in the following year large numbers moved into the central parts of the city. They were spotted at Lock View Road (Stranmillis), at Great Northern Street (Lisburn Road) and Ormeau Park. One grey was even spotted running across the road at Carlisle Circus. Today (2009) the only place where red squirrels are regularly found is in the centre of Belvoir Park, and this population is under serious threat.[2] In addition to losing what was one of our best-loved woodland animals, we have gained a real pest. Grey squirrels, unlike the reds, have the habit of stripping the bark off young trees, reducing the value of plantations.

If protection for our trees is not as good as we might have hoped, what is happening about tree planting? Are we continuing to plant the saplings that will become the urban forest of the future? Perhaps the enthusiasm for planting and promoting trees that we have witnessed over the last few decades will continue, though some indicators suggest that it is waning. For example, with the growth of the local economy and strengthening of the peace process, central government funding for environmental improvement schemes and community projects has been significantly reduced. Other more unexpected factors have also contributed to a reduction in tree planting, such as the introduction by councils of Compulsory Competitive Tendering (CCT) in the 1990s. This separated staff into 'client' and 'contract' groups in which responsibility for delivering projects, such as tree planting in parks, was lost within maze of paperwork and bureaucracy. The adoption of annualised hours for parks grounds staff, which allowed them to work longer hours during the summer and shorter hours during winter months, was seen as a move that would make parks more efficient. However, an unforeseen consequence was that there was less manpower available during the tree planting season. Another decision that at the time was probably seen to be of no great consequence was the ending in 2000 of the Tree Committee. This has removed a long-term focus for a wide range of statutory organisations to work together to promote trees and become involved in Tree Week. The task ahead of us is apparent when you look at the statistics. Northern Ireland has just 6% tree cover compared to 10% in the Republic of Ireland, 17% in Scotland, 14% in Wales and 8% in England. The European Union average is 36%.[3]

What can we do?

When considering the health of the urban forest perhaps the most important question is to what extent are people involved. With ever-growing public concern about issues such as global warming, the loss of biodiversity and the need for sustainability, people are increasingly taking steps to help the environment. The good news for the urban forest is that the benefits of planting trees are now widely appreciated, and the residents of the city can lead the way.

Tree planting provides an opportunity for residents to create a better future for our city. For those of us who are lucky enough to have gardens, can we give a tree a home? Garden centres can supply a huge range of trees that will satisfy every requirement. We can select a tree for a small garden, for a shady garden, a tree with berries to attract birds or, if you have the space, a tree that will grow tall and become a local landmark. Our families can become more environmentally friendly by making trees a focus of our celebrations. Plant a tree to mark events such as a marriage or the birth of a baby, and if there isn't space by the house, ask if it is possible to sponsor tree planting in a park or open space. At Christmas, why not give friends a living tree as a present?

For anyone wanting to get stuck into projects as part of a team of like-minded enthusiasts, there are environmental charities active in Belfast that organise tree days, volunteering events and training courses.

Companies are increasingly becoming involved in environmental projects through Business in the Community. By joining a Residents' Association or perhaps a Friends' Group at a local park we can contribute to the management of public open spaces. Commenting on planning documents is a positive way of ensuring that issues that concern communities including the protection of trees and parks are taken into account. If you would like more information about the environment and what you can do, take a look at the fact sheets, events and links in the Northern Ireland Environment Link web site at www.nienvironmentlink.org.

The current state of the urban forest is largely the result of the landscape having been managed by generations of people, over hundreds of years. Now it is our responsibility to care for this legacy and plant trees that will form the forest for the future. With ever-increasing evidence of the impact that we all have on the planet, we must learn to live with our environment rather than at the cost of the environment. We can all play a role in shaping the future of Belfast and a good way to start is by discovering what we have. We can find the urban forest on our doorstep, the trees in gardens, on pavements, in parks, school and church grounds. Wherever we live in Belfast we are only a bus ride away from one of our big woods. By using our public spaces, by valuing and adding to our city landscapes, we can keep trees, woods and other aspects of our heritage as living history to be treasured and kept for future generations.

Belvoir Park Primary School Tree Day 2008.

References and notes

NOTE – The Public Record Office of Northern Ireland is abbreviated to PRONI and the Public Record Office in Kew, London, is abbreviated to PRO in the following notes and references.

Chapter 2. A look at the early landscape 1570-1700

1 Ulster by Francis Jobson. Trinity College Dublin manuscripts collection. 1209.17; British Library Maps. Cott. Aug. 1.ii.19. Reference to his map making in Ulster is found in Ernest George Atkinson (ed.), *Calendar of the state papers relating to Ireland of the reign of Elizabeth, 1598, January – 1599, March* (London, 1895), p. 445.

2 Eileen McCracken, *The Irish woods since Tudor Times* (Newton Abbot, 1971); Eileen McCracken, 'The Woodlands of Ulster in the Early Seventeenth Century' *Ulster Journal of Archaeology* 10 (1947), pp16-25; Valerie Hall, 'The vegetational landscape of mid Co. Down over the last half millennium: the documentary evidence.' *Ulster Folklife* 35 (1989) pp 72-85.

3 Map of Belfast Lough attributed to Robert Lythe. National Archive, Kew. MPF. 1/77; R. Dunlop, 'Sixteenth-Century Maps of Ireland' *English Historical Review* 20 (1905), pp 309-337; Anon, *Maps and plans in the Public Record Office 1. British Isles, c. 1410-1860* (London, 1967), p. 553.

4 In 1568 the Lord Deputy was involved in an agreement regarding the castle and manor of Belfast in which Sir Brian MacPhelim O'Neill would give certain undertakings, including cutting wood and bringing it to the waterside where it could be used in making bricks at Carrickfergus. J. C. Beckett and R. E. Glasscock, *Belfast. The origin and growth of an industrial city* (London, 1967), pp. 18-19; The Charter of Carrickfergus included a statement that a license was required for anyone 'born outside the dominions of the crown to cross the water of the town to Belfast for wood, timber or other things.' Kenneth Nicholls, *The Irish Fiants of the Tudor sovereigns. volume 2 1558 – 1586* (Dublin 1994), p. 197; In a letter of 1575 the Earl of Essex explained his proposal to create a small town at Belfast, which he suggested would 'relieve Knockfergus [Carrickfergus] with wood, and horsemen being laid there shall command the plains of Clandeboye'. Also an undated note of this period refers to the need for 10 men to be kept in the castle at Belfast and '20 others might needs be there to keep the passage and furnish Carrickfergus with wood.' Mary O'Dowd (ed.), *Calendar of State Papers Ireland Tudor Period 1571-1575* (Dublin, 2000), pp 832, 888; Correspondence dating from 1581 to 'the Lord of the Woods' stated that 'the mayor and inhabitants of Carrickfergus are to bring home this summer their churches' timber out of the woods of Belfast' Belfast News-Letter 13 February 1818 p. 2.

5 Hans Claude Hamilton (ed.), *Calendar of the state papers relating to Ireland of the reign of Elizabeth. 1588, August – 1592, September* (London, 1885), p. 423.

6 P. Roebuck, 'The making of an Ulster great estate: The Chichesters, barons of Belfast and viscounts of Carrickfergus 1599-1648' *Proceedings of the Royal Irish Academy* C 79 (1979), pp 1-25.

7 Robert M. Young, *Historical notices of old Belfast* (Belfast, 1896), pp 27-28; C. W. Russell and J. P. Prendagast, *Calendar of the state papers relating to Ireland in the reign of James 1. 1608-1610* (London, 1874), pp 88-90.

8 Robert M. Young, *The Town Book of the Corporation of Belfast 1613-1816* (Belfast, 1892), pp 97, 98, 155.

9 Edward Hawkins (ed.), *Travels in Holland the united provinces England Scotland and Ireland by Sir William Brereton, Bart* (London, 1844), p. 128; George Benn, *A history of the town of Belfast* (Belfast, 1877), p. 292; S. Shannon Millin, *Additional sidelights on Belfast history* (Belfast, 1938), p. 40.

10 D. A. Chart, 'The break-up of the estate of Con O'Neill, Castlereagh, County Down' *Proceedings of the Royal Irish Academy* 48 (1942), pp 119-151.

11 The Raven Maps. Created by Thomas Raven (c.1574-c.1640), Compact disk digitised by North Down Heritage Centre (Bangor, 2003).

12 The innermost ring of the oldest tree identified at Belvoir dated to 1642. This is given in David Brown and Mike Baillie, 'How old is that oak?' in Ben Simon (ed.), *A Treasured Landscape. The heritage of Belvoir Park* (Belfast, 2005), pp. 85-97. Due to an oversight for which I apologize in the introduction to this book the tree is incorrectly said to date from 1641.

13 George Benn, *A history of the town of Belfast* (Belfast, 1877), p. 146

14 Trevor Carleton, 'Aspects of local history in Malone, Belfast' *Ulster Journal of Archaeology* 39 (1976), pp 62-67.

15 Enrolment of settlement. Exemplification of grant. Various manors in Co Antrim. Lough Neagh and the Bann. PRONI D/389/9; Rt. Hon. Arthur, Earl of Donegall to Sir Wm. Hicks and Sir Audley Mervin Lease for a year from 1 May 1670 PRONI D/509/24; Although no evidence has been found to the enclosure of all of the demesne lands, one reference to an impaled park called 'Cromock parke' has been noted, see Recovery Earl of Donegall common pleas judgment roll 1692. Transcript in PRONI D/34466/2/3.

16 Richard Dobbs, 'Description of the county of Antrim' in G. Hill, *An historical account of the Macdonnells of Antrim* (Belfast, 1873), p. 385; Trevor Carleton, 'Aspects of local history in Malone, Belfast' *Ulster Journal of Archaeology* 39 (1976), pp 62-67.

17 Robert Pentland Mahaffy (ed.), *Calendar of the state papers relating to Ireland of the reign of Charles 1. 1625-1632* (London, 1900), p. 301.

18 Robert Pentland Mahaffy (ed.), *Calendar of the state papers relating to Ireland of the reign of Charles 1. 1625-163* (London, 1900), pp 515-516.

19 Robert Pentland Mahaffy (ed.), *Calendar of the state papers relating to Ireland of the reign of Charles 1. 1625-1632* (London, 1900), p. 541.

20 Robert Pentland Mahaffy (ed.), *Calendar of the state papers relating to Ireland preserved in the Public Record Office. 1663-1665* (London, 1907), pp 647, 648.

21 Robert Pentland Mahaffy (ed.), *Calendar of state papers relating to Ireland preserved in the Public Record Office. 1669-1670* (London, 1910), pp 72-73.

22 S. Shannon Millin, *Additional sidelights on Belfast History* (Belfast, 1938) p. 4, 8.

23 Enrolment of settlement. Exemplification of grant. Various manors in Co Antrim. Lough Neagh and the Bann. 20 July 1670 PRONI D/389/9; Lease of 125 acres for 61 years from 1 November 1691. Rt. Hon. Anne Countess of Longford and her trustees to Elizabeth Fletcher, Belfast New Enclosures. Parish of Belfast. 4 January 1692. PRONI D/412/2.

24 Assignment of leases of lands containing 188 acres. Consideration £165. John Fletcher to Wm. Lockheart and Wm. Crafford all of Belfast. New Inclosures, Mankin's Copse, Foster's Land, Rory's Land. Parish of Belfast 1 December 1688. PRONI D/412/1.

25 Séamus Pender (ed.), *A census of Ireland, circa 1659* (Dublin, 1939), p. 8; Enrolment of settlement. Exemplification of grant. Various manors in Co Antrim. Lough Neagh and the Bann. 20 July 1670 PRONI D/389/9; See also Deidre Morton, 'Former townland names in Tuath Cinament' *Bulletin of the Ulster place-name society* 5 (1957), pp 46-53.

26 George Benn, *A history of the town of Belfast from 1799 till 1810. Incidental notices on local topics.* Volume II (Belfast, 1880), p. 147.

27 Edward Hawkins (ed.), *Travels in Holland the united provinces England Scotland and Ireland by Sir William Brereton, Bart* (London, 1844), p. 129; W. Reeves, 'Irish itinerary of Father Edmund MacCana' *Ulster Journal of Archaeology* 2 (1854), pp 44-59; Robert C. Simington, *The Civil Survey 1654-6* Vol. X. Miscellanea (Dublin, 1961), p. 67. The Civil Survey for Castlereagh attributed the lack of woodland to it having been 'destroyed by the Rebellion', though this seems unlikely.

28 Recovery Earl of Donegall common pleas judgement roll 1692. PRONI D/3466/2/3.

29 D. A. Chart, 'The break-up of the estate of Con O'Neill, Castlereagh, County Down' *Proceedings of the Royal Irish Academy* 48 (1942), pp 119-151.

30 Eileen McCracken, 'The Woodlands of Ulster in the Early Seventeenth Century' *Ulster Journal of Archaeology* 10 (1947), pp 16-25.

31 Kenneth Nicholls, 'Woodland cover in pre-Modern Ireland' in Patrick J. Duffy, David Edwards and Elizabeth FitzPatrick (eds), *Gaelic Ireland c. 1250 - c. 1650 Land, Lordship and Settlement* (Ireland, 2001), p. 201.

32 Henry Joy, *Historical collections relative to the town of Belfast* (Belfast, 1817), pp 16-19; George Benn, *A history of the town of Belfast* (Belfast, 1877), pp 334-335; David Brown and Mike Baillie, 'How old is that oak?' in Ben Simon (ed.), *A Treasured Landscape. The heritage of Belvoir Park* (Belfast, 2005), pp 85-97.

33 J. H. Andrews, 'Notes on the historical geography of the Irish iron industry' *Irish geography* 3 (1956) pp 139-149; Eileen McCracken, *The Irish woods since Tudor Times* (Newton Abbot 1971).

34 The setting up of ironworks to improve land for agriculture is suggested by a proposal to establish an ironworks at Killultagh to make the area a 'good, pleasant and flourishing country' R. P. Mahaffy (ed.), *Calendar of the state papers relating to Ireland of the reign of Charles I. 1625-1632* (London, 1900), p. 516. Conditions attached to an agreement of 1673 for the supply of wood for an ironworks from the Brownlow estate of north Armagh indicate that in this instance the ironworks was established to generate income from trees of no timber value while also clearing scrub. See R. G. Gillespie (ed.), *Settlement and survival on an Ulster Estate. The Brownlow Leasebook 1667-171* (Belfast, 1988), pp 122-123. It is possible that some ironworks did not clear woods but sustainably managed trees by coppicing to provide a long term supply of wood (see Oliver Rackham, 'Looking for ancient woodland in Ireland' in Jon R. Pilcher and Séan. S. Mac an tSaoir (eds) *Wood, trees and forests in Ireland* (Dublin,1995), pp 1-12). However, in this study of NE Ireland the only evidence noted that might possibly support this is an advertisement which informs us that a coppice existed by an ironworks at Castledawson (Belfast News Letter 26 June 1750 p. 3).

35 R. G. Gillespie (ed.), *Settlement and survival on an Ulster Estate. The Brownlow Leasebook 1667-1711* (Belfast, 1988)

36 C. W. Russell and J. P. Prendagast (eds), *Calendar of the state papers relating to Ireland in the reign of James 1. 1608-1610* (London, 1874), p. 356.

37 S. Shannon Millin, *Additional sidelights on Belfast History* (Belfast, 1938), p. 4.

38 Robert Pentland Mahaffy (ed.), *Calendar of the state papers relating to Ireland preserved in the Public Records Office. 1647-1660* (London, 1908), pp 394-395.

39 R. G. Gillespie (ed.), *Settlement and survival on an Ulster Estate. The Brownlow Leasebook 1667-1711* (Belfast, 1988).

40 Indenture between Arthur Earl of Donegall and Thomas Waring dated 1st November 1659. Referred to in the Benn papers PRONI D/3113/4/12.

41 Lease of 125 acres for 61 years from 1 November 1691. Rt. Hon. Anne Countess of Longford and her trustees to Elizabeth Fletcher, Belfast. New Enclosures. Parish of Belfast. 4 January 1692. PRONI D/412/2; Rt. Hon. Anne, Countess of Longford, Sir Richard Cox and James McCartney, Belfast to John Carr, Old Park, Belfast. Lease of 23 acres for 61 years from 1 November 1691 PRONI D/509/30.

42 Richard Dobbs, 'Description of the county of Antrim' in G. Hill, *An historical account of the Macdonnells of Antrim.* (Belfast, 1873), p. 385

43 R. G. Gillespie (ed.), *Settlement and survival on an Ulster Estate. The Brownlow Leasebook 1667-1711* (Belfast, 1988).

44 Robert Pentland Mahaffy (ed.), *Calendar of the state papers relating to Ireland preserved in the Public Records Office. 1663-1665* (London, 1907), p. 441.

45 Robert Pentland Mahaffy (ed.), *Calendar of the state papers relating to Ireland preserved in the Public Records Office. 1663-1665* (London, 1907), p. 648; Robert Pentland Mahaffy (ed.) *Calendar of the state papers relating to Ireland preserved in the public records office. 1666-1669* (London, 1908), pp 473, 587, 693.

46 E. St John Brooks, *Sir Hans Sloane* (London, 1954); E. Charles Nelson, 'Sir Arthur Rawdon (1662-1695) of Moira: his life and letters, family and friends, and his Jamaican plants' *Belfast Natural History and Philosophical Society Proceedings* 10 (1981), pp 30-52; Keith Lamb and Patrick Bowe, *A history of gardening in Ireland* (Dublin, 1995), pp 24-25.

47 Castleward Letters. Book 2 page 95, letter dated 15th November 1725. PRONI MIC/596.

48 John Dubourdieu, *Statistical survey of County Antrim* (Dublin, 1812), pp 286-287.

49 Measurements of the trees are from – John Templeton's diary, manuscript in Ulster Museum; John Dubourdieu *Statistical survey of County Antrim.* (Dublin, 1812), p. 287; J. C. Loudon, *Arboretum et fruticetum Britannicum* volume 1 (London, 1838), p. 112; C. Douglas Deane, *The Ulster Countryside.* (Belfast, 1983), pp 52-53; Ben Simon (ed.), *A Treasured Landscape. The heritage of Belvoir Park* (Belfast, 2005), p. 161. Only two trees were mentioned in a note about the site published in the Belfast Telegraph 10 February 1945 p. 4.

Chapter 3. Trees in a developing town 1700-1800

1 Earl of Donegall. Accounts of payments and receipts. 1706-1715. Transcript at PRONI T/455/1-2. PRONI copy of originals are at MIC/4B/1.

2 S. Shannon Millin, *Additional sidelights on Belfast history* (Belfast, 1938), p. 43; Raymond Gillespie, *Early Belfast* (Belfast, 2007), pp 152-154.

3 Earl of Donegall. Accounts of payments and receipts. 1706-1715. PRONI T/455/1-2.

4 S. Shannon Millin, *Additional sidelights on Belfast history* (Belfast, 1938), pp 46-48; Initial uncertainty about the future of the castle site in the years following the fire is also shown by a note on the Linenhall Library manuscript map of Belfast by John Maclanachan (c. 1715). In this map the castle site is shown blank and the note explains that he '....omitted the castle till I see how it may be repaired.' See Linenhall Library list of maps number 34.

5 Earl of Donegall. Accounts of payments and receipts. 1706-1715. PRONI T/455/1-2.

6 For references the castle site see Chancery papers: Donegall estate. PRONI T/3425/3. For repair of walls and gate see for example T/3425/3/11/21; T/3425/3/12/35-37, 41-44, 45-46. Repair of Lord Donegall's house in Belfast see for example T/3425/3/9 5-6, 9, 32-33.; T/3425/3/10/23; T/3425/3/11/15, 36; T/3425/3/12/38-40; T/3425/3/14/24, 26-30. Rebuilding of Donegall's house see for example T/3425/3/16/67, 88-90; T/3425/3/17/58-59. The house being repaired (Donegall's house) is referred to as being in the castle court in T/3425/3/16/92-94 and see T/3425/3/16/82-84 where bricks 'for Belfast house' were delivered to the castle yard; S. Shannon Millin, 'Story of Belfast Castle fire tragedy.' Belfast Telegraph 14 August 1934 p. 11 suggests that Lord Donegall's house was a former coach house. He gives a date for a rebuilding in 1787 though does not provide evidence. George Benn gives some information about this building in *A history of the town of Belfast.* (Belfast, 1877), pp 551-552 and in volume 2 (Belfast, 1880), pp 115-116.

7 George T. Stokes (ed.), *Pococke's tour in Ireland in 1752.* (Dublin, 1891), p. 21.

8 Advertisement in Belfast News-Letter 10-14 May 1782 p. 1.

9 George Benn, *A history of the town of Belfast* (Belfast, 1877), pp 550-551.

10 Trees by auction. Belfast News-Letter 26-30 March 1784 p. 3; To be sold by public auction. Belfast News-Letter 10-14 September 1784 p. 3; Elm and ash trees by auction. Belfast News-Letter 6-10 April 1795 p. 3; It is perhaps worth noting that none of there trees were beech, a species that John Dubourdieu, *Statistical survey of the County of Antrim* (Dublin 1812) p. 289 referred to as having been a notable feature of the castle gardens.

11 Article by H. Joy Belfast News-Letter 13 February 1818 p. 2.

12 Article by Colin Johnston Robb Belfast Telegraph 31 October 1949 p. 4. The source of the information quoted in this article is not known.

13 Earl of Donegall. Accounts of payments and receipts. 1706-1715. PRONI T/455/1-2.

14 Chancery papers: Donegall estate. PRONI T/3425/3/14/82.

15 Advertisement in Belfast News-Letter 20 April 1753 p. 2.

16 Advertisement in Belfast News-Letter 9 July 1765 p. 3; 14 December 1770 p. 3; 31 May 1771 p. 2.

17 Leases of lands at Cromac Wood, 14 December 1770 at PRONI. Rt Hon. Arthur Chichester Earl of Donegall to Waddell Cunningham D/509/552; to James Henderson D/509/ 554; to George Portis D/509/556. The same conditions also applied to leases of 1770 for land between Cromac and the castle gardens, see D/509/553.

18 Advertisement in Belfast News-Letter 28 May 1773 p. 3. This was described in a later advertisement (19-22 April 1774 p. 2) as being 'next the Plains' (ie southern part of Cromac).

19 To be sold by auction. Belfast News-Letter 18-21 April 1786 p. 3; 11-15 August 1786 p. 1.

20 A map of the town and environs of Belfast. Surveyed in 1791 by James Williamson. Reproduced in Raymond Gillespie and Stephen A. Royle *Belfast Part 1, to 1840* Irish historic town atlas 12, Royal Irish Academy (Dublin, 2003); A copy of a more detailed map of part of Cromac, surveyed by James Williamson in 1793, is preserved in PRONI T/1129/424. This shows tall spaced trees along some hedge lines and a few trees remaining in a field near the 'Pass Loning', in an area described in the key as wood.

21 Advertisement for Cromack Wood Farm. Belfast News-Letter 24-27 May 1791 p. 3.

22 Charles Abbot, *Journal of a tour in Ireland and north Wales* (1792,

Manuscript in National Archives, Kew) PRO 30/9/23 p. 67; George Benn, *The History of the Town of Belfast* (Belfast, 1823) p. 165.

23 An article by 'S. M. S.' in the Northern Whig 24 February 1837 p. 4 mentions felling at Glenarm in 1753 and the construction of the *Shillelagh* from the timber in 1793. Evidence for felling around 1753 can perhaps be tentatively inferred from the fact that in this year an advertisement for the sale of woods in the Great Deer Park at Glenarm was placed in the Belfast News-Letter (7 August 1753 p. 3). Good evidence for extensive felling towards the end of the century is provided by the observations of Charles Abbot, *Journal of a tour in Ireland and north Wales* (1792, Manuscript in National Archives, Kew) PRO 30/9/23 p. 74 who mentioned that at the Deer Park 'a very flourishing wood of Timber Trees was cut down this Season' and by John Templeton's diary (preserved in the Ulster Museum), entry for 28 August 1810.

24 John Moore Johnston, *Heterogenea, or medley. For the benefit of the poor* (Downpatrick, 1803), p. 214. An advertisement for the sale of materials from the stables of Portmore in 1756 (Belfast News-Letter 4 June 1756 p. 2) may indicate that the dismantling of the estate started a few years earlier than suggested by John Moore Johnston.

25 Earl of Donegall. Accounts of payments and receipts. 1706-1715. PRONI T/455/1-2.

26 Chancery papers: Donegall estate. PRONI. See for example T/3425/3/9/10; T/3425/3/14/38-39; T/3425/3/16/68-70.

27 Advertisement in Belfast News-Letter 13 May 1766 p. 2.

28 Earl of Donegall. Accounts of payments and receipts. 1706-1715. PRONI T/455/1-2; It is interesting to speculate if William Dumbill (Dumville?) was related to John Dumville, a Cheshire man, who had been employed to keep game and look after the woods at the Conway estate at Portmore. See R. P. Mahaffy (ed.), *Calendar of the state papers relating to Ireland preserved in the Public Record Office 1663-1665* (London, 1907), pp. 523, 633 and R. P. Mahaffy (ed.), *Calendar of the state papers relating to Ireland preserved in the Public Record Office 1647-1660* (London,1908), p. 650.

29 Chancery papers: Donegall estate. See for example PRONI T/3425/3/9/11; T/3425/3/11/9-14; T/3425/3/12/20-22; T/3425/3/13/35-36.

30 Chancery papers: Donegall estate. PRONI T/3425/3/11/55; T/3425/3/12/8; T/3425/3/12/27-28; T/3425/3/11/5-8.

31 Chancery papers: Donegall estate. PRONI T/3525/3/16/95-96; David Dickson, *Artic Ireland* (Belfast, 1997). Notice for Grazing let in the deer park see Belfast News-Letter 4-8 May 1795 p. 1.

32 Robert M. Young (ed.), *Historical notices of old Belfast* (Belfast, 1896), p. 156. The reference to a fountain may perhaps have been a spring or the well now known as the Volunteers Well.

33 Chancery papers: Donegall estate. The 1736 reference is in PRONI T/3425/3/12/35-37. The 1735 reference was seen in the original papers at PRO at Kew but is missing from the PRONI copies.

34 P. Sandby, *The virtuosi's museum: containing select views, in England, Scotland and Ireland* (London, 1778), plate CII; The painting by John Nixon is reproduced on the cover of the book by Eamon Phoenix, *Two acres of Irish History. A study through time of Friar's Bush and Belfast 1570-1918* Ulster Historical Foundation (Belfast, 1988).

35 Article in the Belfast News-Letter 16-19 February 1790 p. 3; George Benn, *The History of the Town of Belfast*. (Belfast, 1823), p. 165.

36 See for example the views of Belfast shipyards and Cave Hill reproduced in Eileen McCracken, *The Irish Woods since Tudor Times* (Newton Abbot 1971) pp 34, 85.

37 See Appendix 1.

38 An advertisement in the Belfast News-Letter of 2 October 1750 p. 3 for a timber sale at Rose Hall near Banbridge mentions John Nicholson, 'Clerk of the Woods'. A later advertisement for the felling of trees at this site in the Belfast News-Letter of 18 May 1753 p. 2 mentions attendance in the wood being given by George Taylor 'Clerk of the Groves'. In the early 18th century Richard Millhouse was 'Clerk to the woods' near Portmore (Killultagh) see *Letter book of Issac McCartney 1704-1707* p. 364 PRONI D/501/1. In a sale of coppice wood at Castledawson advertised in the Belfast News-Letter on 26 June 1750 p. 3 it was said that 'Constant attendance will be given by a Clerk who will sell the same.' These clerks were most likely responsible for keeping accounts of income and expenditure for these woods.

39 Edward Wakefield, *An account of Ireland, statistical and political* (London, 1812), volume 1. p. 536.

40 Chancery papers: Donegall estate. PRONI T/3425/3/9/2; Robert M. Young, *The town book of the Corporation of Belfast, 1613-1816* (Belfast, 1892), p. 339.

41 Terence Reeves-Smyth 'The Natural History of Demesnes' in John

Wilson Foster and Helena C. G. Chesney (eds) *Nature in Ireland. A scientific and cultural history* (Dublin, 1997), pp 549-572.

42 Ben Simon (ed.), *A treasured landscape. The heritage of Belvoir Park* (Belfast, 2005) Chapter 2.

43 Advertisement in Belfast News-Letter 2-5 March 1784 p. 4.

44 WM. D. D. Henry, manuscript in Armagh Public Library (1739) ISBN P00194176X p. 149.

45 George T. Stokes, *Pococke's tour in Ireland in 1752* (Dublin, 1891), p. 19; Anon, *The ancient and present state of the County of Down* (Dublin, 1774) p. 60.

46 Advertisements concerning theft and damage of statuary at Moira are in Belfast News-Letter 27 February 1756 p. 2, 29 April 1762 p. 3, 15-18 March 1791 p.1. Concerning Purdysburn 16-20 July 1773 p. 2.

47 Anon, *A topographical and chorographical survey of the County of Down*. (Dublin, 1740), p. 29. This important early account of County Down, generally attributed to Charles Smith, is not well known and has only been noted by the author since the publication of 'A treasured landscape'.

48 Ben Simon (ed.), *A treasured landscape. The heritage of Belvoir Park* (Belfast, 2005) Chapter 2.

49 Indenture dated 26 March 1712 between Roger Haddock and James Willson. PRONI D/971/42/A/15/2; Anon, *A topographical and chorographical survey of the County of Down*. (Dublin, 1740), p. 29; The carved stone was noticed by the author in 2007. A sample was taken in March 2007 from a felled oak by the path close to the old ice house at location 334089 368124. The oak tree was kindly dated by David Brown at the Palaeoecology Centre, Queen's University, sample number Q10906. The centre of the tree was present and it dated from 1737; Conveyance, James Willson of Purdysburn to Hill Willson, his son. 30 September 1741. PRONI D/971/42/A/15/4.

50 Unfortunately no early descriptions of the grounds have been found and the age of the former yew hedges is not known, though visitors to the area in the 1867 considered the hedges a remarkable feature and noted that they were reputedly 'old in Cromwell's time'. (Annual Report of the Belfast Naturalists' Field Club 5 (1868) pp13-15). Although this comment is clearly fanciful, it does suggest that the yews were by then a well established feature, planted perhaps in the 18th rather than 19th century.

51 Valuations of timber at Purdysburn. 1802-1808. PRONI D/971/42/A/15/52-59.

52 Ben Simon, unpublished survey of lowland wood pasture in Belfast (2008) Copies available from the Forest of Belfast. In contrast to the widely spaced parkland trees around the house, an advertisement in the Belfast News-Letter 25 October 1805 p.1 concerning lands at Purdysburn demesne referred to the 'Purdysburn River, over which hangs a richly wooded bank'.

53 Peter Rankin (ed.), *Malone House* Ulster Architectural Heritage Association (Belfast, 1983).

54 Map of Malone Estate PRONI D/915/18/1 This document is missing from PRONI. A PRONI photocopy of the original is held by Belfast Parks and a slide of the map and list of the field names is at PRONI T/1965/1A/11 and 12.

55 Advertisement, Belfast News-Letter 19-22 March 1782 p. 1.

56 Anon, *The ancient and present state of the County of Down* (Dublin, 1744), p. 69. The impressive speed of this development was perhaps in part due to the use of a flat roof for the mansion house though the author seems to have doubted its suitability noting 'A little Time will shew whether this sort of roofing will answer the purpose in this moist Climate'!

57 It is generally considered that Wilmont was created in the early 1760s. See R. Scott, *A breath of fresh air* (Belfast, 2000), p. 112. In early 1970s a sample of oak was collected by Queen's University from a recently felled oak at Wilmont (Q531). The centre of the tree was present and it dated from 1777. A sample was taken in February 2006 from a fallen oak in the wood by the path that parallels the River Lagan at location 330360 367564. The oak tree was kindly dated by David Brown at the Palaeoecology Centre, Queen's University, sample number Q10797. The centre of the tree was present. It dated from 1775.

58 William Shaw Mason, *A statistical account, or parochial survey of Ireland* (Dublin, 1814-1819), volume 3, p 186.

59 George Taylor, *Taylor and Skinner's maps of the roads of Ireland surveyed in 1777* (London, 1778).

60 Advertisement in Belfast News-Letter 2-5 December 1777 p. 3.

61 Although there is little evidence for coppicing in the Belfast region at this time, there are indications that it was widespread elsewhere. For example see Arthur Wollaston Hutton, *Arthur Young's tour in Ireland (1776-1779)* (London, 1892) p. 90 and advertisements such as the

sale of 'any Quantity of grey Salley Hoops of the growth of three years…the whole plantation containing 24 acres' in the Toome area, Belfast News-Letter 3 October 1760 p. 2; the 'large parcel of osiers' offered for sale at Downpatrick, Belfast News-Letter 17 June 1757 p. 2; and the sale of 'all the Underwood in that Coppice, commonly known by the Name of the double Coppice' near Castledawson, Belfast News-Letter 26-29 August 1777 p. 3.

62 Castleward Papers. Original only available as poor quality copies in PRONI MIC/596. Book 1. pp 174, 176. See also PRONI D/2092/1/1.

63 Anon, *A topographical and chorographical survey of the County of Down.* (Dublin, 1740), p. 44.

64 See for example Rt Hon. Arthur Earl of Donegall to Wm Montgomery, Corran, Larne. Lease of 1st Nov. 1742 PRONI D/509/53.

65 See for example Rt. Hon. Arthur Earl of Donegall to John Brown, Belfast. Lease of 20 June 1770 PRONI D/509/441.

66 Advertisement in Belfast News-Letter 4 February 1775 p. 3; 20 January 1761 p. 2.

67 S. M'Skimin, *The history and antiquities of the county of the town of Carrickfergus* (Belfast, 1811), p. 118; John Dubourdieu, *Statistical survey of County Antrim* (Dublin, 1812) pp 158-160.

68 Advertisement in Belfast News-Letter 2 January 1761 p. 2.

69 Richard R. Cherry, *The Irish land law and land purchase acts 1860-1901.* third edition (Dublin, 1903), pp 355-360, 414-416; See also reports of court judgments referring to townparks in the *Irish Law Times*, in particular the review on pp 16-17 and reports on pp 2, 4 in 1883.

70 Advertisement in Belfast News-Letter 4 May 1764 p. 3, 8 May 1764 p. 3; Belfast Commercial Chronicle 4 April 1807 p. 2, 25 March 1812 p. 1.

71 Note in Belfast News-Letter 8 March 1850 p. 2.

Chapter 4. The first great tree planting project

1 Advertisements in Belfast News-Letter 28 December 1756 p. 3, 6 April 1756 p. 3 and 27 August 1756 p. 2.

2 Eileen McCracken, 'Notes on Eighteenth Century Irish Nurserymen' *Irish Forestry* 24 (1967) pp 39-58.

3 Eileen and Donal McCracken, *A register of trees for County Londonderry, 1768-1911* PRONI (Belfast, 1984), pp 1-15; Eoin Neeson, *A history of Irish forestry* (Dublin, 1991), pp 301- 308.

4 Advertisement in Belfast News-Letter 25 March 1766 p. 2.

5 Eileen and Donal McCracken, *A register of trees for County Londonderry, 1768-1911* PRONI (Belfast, 1984), pp 1-15.

6 Castleward Papers. Only available as poor quality copies in PRONI MIC/596. Book 2. p. 76. See also PRONI D/2092/1/2.

7 Eoin Neeson, *A history of Irish forestry* (Dublin, 1991), pp 92-95, 309-318.

8 Anon, 'Premiums offered by the Dublin Society.' *Royal Dublin Society transactions* 5 (1806), pp 41-141; Meeting of the Dublin Society, *Royal Dublin Society proceedings* 2 (1766), p. 315, 319, 357.

9 Example of notices placed in the Belfast News-Letter include: Farmers Society of the four Lower Baronies of the County of Antrim, 18 April 1775 p. 3, 14 October 1755 p. 2, 16 February 1758 p. 3; Downe Society for the Encouragement of Agriculture and other useful Arts, 9 July 1756 p. 2, 2 November 1756 p. 3; Ballymoney Club, 23-26 December 1788 p. 3; Farming Society for Carrickfergus and Kilroot Parishes, 11 March 1803 p. 3; Lower Massereene and Glenavy Farming Society, 26 April 1803 p. 3, 6 July 1804 p. 3.

10 Examples of advertisements of cottage industry sales of trees from the Belfast News-Letter: Edward Ross of Lisburn sells young ash trees, 4 March 1760 p. 3; Edward Maze of Ballinderry sells thorns, young fir and apple trees, 5 February 1773 p. 3; John Dow at Drumbo Bridge has young oaks for sale, 4-7 February 1777 p. 1; William Christian of Glenavy has thorn and crab quicks and a few apple trees for sale, growing in his garden, 28 February - 4 March 1783 p. 3.

11 Examples of advertisements in the Belfast News-Letter: Samuel Pue, 26 January 1749 p. 3; James Sloan, 18 December 1750 p. 4, 26 December 1758 p. 2, William Dick, 28 January 1755 p. 3; George Cutler, 25 September 1759 p. 3.

12 Examples of advertisements in the Belfast News-Letter: John Wallice of Holymount, 3 January 1764 p. 3, 13 January 1769 p. 3, 29 January 1773 p. 3; William Dickie (perhaps the same person as William Dick) regularly advertised his Armagh nursery eg 20 January 1761 p. 2, 21 February 1764 p. 4, 4 August 1772 p. 3, 2 March 1773

p. 2; David Wilkie of Moira, 23 January 1767 p. 2, 21 August 1767 p. 2, 14 March 1769 p. 1, 14-17 February 1792 p. 3 and Alexander Cooper of Sheanogstown, 24 March 1767 p. 2, 10 November 1767 p. 1, 17 November 1769 p. 3.

13 Examples of advertisements in the Belfast News-Letter: William Johnson, 10 March 1761 p. 2, 7 October 1768 p. 2, 27 October 1772 p. 1, 26-29 March 1782 p. 2, 8 December 1791 p. 3; Arthur Johnson, 11 March 1760 p. 2, 6 December 1768 p. 1, 22-25 January 1782 p. 3.

14 Advertisements in the Belfast News-Letter, 15-18 February 1774 p. 3, 28-31 March 1775 p. 2.

15 Advertisement in the Belfast News-Letter 13-16 January 1776 p. 2.

16 Anon, 'Premiums offered and adjudged by the Dublin Society' *Royal Dublin Society Transactions* 5 (1806), pp 41-141; William Bell's nursery see for example advertisements in the Belfast News-Letter 19-22 February 1782 p. 3, 7-11 March 1783 p. 3, 26-30 November 1790 p. 3.

17 Belfast News-Letter: David Hervey takes over nursery 14 February 1800 p. 3; Death notice of William Bell 26 February 1805 p. 3; Death of David Hervey and Elisabeth Bell continues seed shop 6 November 1810 p. 3.

18 John Hervey's business see for example advertisements in Belfast News-Letter of 10 January 1815 p. 3, 7 March 1815 p. 3, 23 December 1817 p. 1, 5 December 1826 p. 3. Note about Irish yew in *Gardener's Magazine* 2 (1827), p. 356. Article 'Affecting case of Hydrophobia' in Northern Whig 5 October 1829 p. 4.

19 John Bullen's business see for example advertisements in Belfast News-Letter of 23-27 December 1791 p. 1, 1 February 1799 p. 4, 2 March 1804 p. 3. The fate of the nursery is given in Anon, *A popular guide to the Royal Botanic Garden of Belfast* (Belfast, 1851), p. viii.

20 Daniel Robertson's business see for example advertisements in Belfast-News Letter of 15 October 1799 p. 3, 7 March 1800 p. 3, 20 February 1801 pp 1 and 3, 7 February 1804 p. 3, 14 December 1810 p. 3.

21 Edward Lindsay's business see for example advertisements in Belfast-News Letter 15-19 February 1796 p. 3, 23-27 January 1797 p. 3, 14 February 1800 p. 3, 9 June 1801 p. 4, 23 February 1802 p. 2, 10 January 1806 p. 3, 25 December 1807 p. 3, 13 May 1808 p. 3, 1 March 1811 p. 1, 15 November 1814 p. 3, 25 Feb 1834 p. 3. The business was taken over by his son, Edward junior, who sold the stock and tried to sell the nursery site in Malone for a cemetery.

22 Advertisement in Belfast News-Letter 25 February 1840 p. 3.

23 Richard and William Penton's business see for example advertisements in Belfast News-Letter 3-7 November 1775 p. 4, 3 March 1802 p. 3, 1 February 1803 p. 3, 26 November 1811 p. 3, 27 October 1815 p. 3.

24 Advertisements in Belfast News-Letter of 26 January 1749 p. 3, 21 April 1767 p. 3, 14 March 1769 p. 1.

25 Advertisements in Belfast News-Letter of 7 April 1772 p. 1, 16 October 1772 p. 1; 1-4 January 1782 p. 3, 20-24 March 1789 p. 3. See also John Dubourdieu, *Statistical Survey of the County of Down* (Dublin, 1802) p. 61.

26 Advertisements in Belfast News-Letter: Kenneth Sutherland, 18-21 March 1777 p. 3; R. O'Donnell 4 March 1801 p. 1; William Pink, 11 January 1814 p. 3. For reference to Kenneth Sutherland of Belvoir see Ben Simon (ed.), *A treasured landscape. The heritage of Belvoir Park* (Belfast, 2005) p. 143, reference 31.

27 Advertisements in Belfast News-Letter: Dan O'Brien, 16 October 1772 p. 3 and 3-7 February 1775 p. 3; Dutton, 24 February 1801 p. 3; Pat Purfield, 26 August 1808 p. 1. Mr Dutton was without doubt Hely Dutton, the landscape gardener.

Chapter 5. Views of Victorian Belfast

1 George Benn, *The History of the Town of Belfast* (Belfast, 1823), p. 165.

2 See tree records in Dublin Gazette summarised in Appendix 3.

3 Based on the tree planting records summarised in Appendix 3.

4 Eileen and Donal McCracken, *A register of trees for County Londonderry, 1768-1911* (Belfast, 1984), pp 9-10.

5 Advertisement in Belfast News-Letter 5 October 1868 p. 2.

6 James Fraser, *Hand Book for travellers in Ireland* (Dublin, 1859), p. 181.

7 Henry Bayly, *A topographical and historical account of Lisburn* (Belfast, 1834), p. 69.

8 A sample was taken in 2006 from a felled oak at the northern end of the park, at the boundary between the park and Queen's University playing fields. The tree was one of a number that form a conspicuous row of oaks. Location 331941 369293. The oak tree was kindly dated by David Brown at the Palaeoecology Centre, Queen's University,

sample number Q10796. The centre of the tree was present. It dated from 1810.

9 A. Atkinson, *Ireland exhibited to England* (London, 1823), pp 34-35.

10 Peter Rankin, (ed.), *Malone House* Ulster Architectural Heritage Association (Belfast, 1983); The inconvenience caused by the moving of the road was the subject of an article in the Northern Whig 13 August 1829 p. 2.

11 Map of Malone Demesne in the Parish of Belfast and County of Antrim belonging to William Legge. Surveyed by Thomas Pattison Sen. and Junr. 1825 PRONI D/915/18/9; Ben Simon, unpublished survey of lowland wood pasture in Belfast (2008) Copies available from the Forest of Belfast; Appendix 4.

12 Advertisement in Belfast News-Letter 19 May 1809 p. 1; Ben Simon (ed.), *A treasured landscape. The heritage of Belvoir Park* (Belfast, 2005), chapter 2. An interesting feature of Belvoir are cedars and other exotic specimen trees in the garden and around the demesne. These are thought to have been planted by the Batesons though an 1820 advertisement for the sale of timber at Belvoir including a large acacia tree (Belfast News-Letter 25 April 1820 p. 1) suggests that some exotics were being grown in the 18th century.

13 For the history of the estate see R. Scott, *A breath of fresh air. The story of Belfast's parks* (Belfast, 2000), pp 111-115; Linenhall Library map collection, 'Map of Wilmont situate in the parish of Drumbeg and counties of Antrim and Down the property of James Stewart Esq. by Robt. Pattison 1842'; Angélique Day and Patrick McWilliams, *Ordnance Survey Memoirs of Ireland. Parishes of County Antrim II 1832-8 Lisburn and south Antrim.* 8 (Belfast, 1991), pp 125-126.

14 See Appendix 3.

15 The proposed division of the demesne is shown on Linenhall Library map collection, Map of Wilmont demesne, the property of Alexander Mackenzie Shaw Esq. situate in the barony of Upper Belfast and County of Antrim. Surveyed valued and divided into lots by John Irwine Whitty LLD CE 15 Henrietta Street Dublin, 1854.

16 Two samples was taken in 2007 from felled trees at Stranmillis, an oak by a circular building towards the east of the campus (333586 371411) felled in 2002 and a sweet chestnut just west of the pond (333379 371153) that staff recalled as having been felled in the mid 1980s. Both had girths of over 3m. The samples were kindly dated by David Brown at the Palaeoecology Centre, Queen's University, sample numbers Q10939 (oak), Q10940 (sweet chestnut). The oak had 136 annual rings, the sweet chestnut 170 annual rings.

17 W. A. Maguire, 'Ormeau house' *Ulster Journal of Archaeology* 42 (1979), pp 66-71.

18 The early history of Ormeau has not been researched in detail. Trees are shown in 'A map of the Town & Environs of Belfast Taken to the Distance of One Irish Mile from the Exchange. Surveyed in 1791 by James Williamson'.

19 Phillip Dixon Hardy, *The Northern tourist* (Dublin, 1830), p. 208; Henry Heaney (ed.), *A Scottish Whig in Ireland 1835-38. The Irish Journals of Robert Graham of Redgorton* (Dublin, 1999), p. 350.

20 See Appendix 3 for reference to planting by Will. Irvin, 1801; Rt. Hon. Arthur, Earl of Donegall to William Irvin. Counterpart lease for 21 years, Cromac Wood, Belfast. 1 May 1786. PRONI D/509/672.

21 Thomas D. Hincks, 'Memoir of the late John Templeton Esq.' *Magazine of natural history* 1 (1829), pp 403-406, 496; 2 (1829) pp 305-310.

22 The diary of John Templeton. Manuscript. Ulster Museum

23 James Crow, Maps of the Donegall estate in Co. Antrim and Co, Down (1767-79). PRONI D/835/1/3/19-21; Trevor Carleton, Aspects of local history in Malone, Belfast *Ulster Journal of Archaeology* 39 (1976) pp 62-67.

24 The diary of John Templeton. Manuscript. Ulster Museum.

25 Anon, 'Tour to the Giant's Causeway.' *Irish Farmers' Journal and Weekly Intelligencer* 4 number 2, 9 September 1815 p. 13, reprinted in Belfast News-Letter 12 September 1815.

26 Thomas D. Hincks, 'Memoir of the late John Templeton Esq.' *Magazine of natural history* 1 (1829) pp 403-406, 496. 2 (1829) pp 305-310; J. C. Loudon, *Arboretum et fruticetum britannicum* Second edition volume 4 (London, 1844), pp 2294-2295; The tree was subsequently referred to in Anon, *A popular guide to the Royal Botanic Garden of Belfast.* (Belfast, 1851), p. vi.

27 Pollution from flax dams for example noted in an article by 'W. R. H.', 'A recent visit to north Ireland' *The Gardeners' Chronicle and Agricultural Gazette* (1866) p. 909 and an article in the Down Recorder 10 November 1900 p. 3. The 'Blacksfaff Nuisance' is graphically described in an article in the Belfast News-Letter 22 September 1855 p 5.

28 Ralph Tate, *Flora Belfastiensis* (Belfast, 1863), p. xiii.

29 Wm. Thompson, *The natural history of Ireland* volume 1 (London, 1849), p. 75, volume 2 (1850), p. 141, volume 4 (1856), p. 9; The heronry at Belvoir is also mentioned by James D. Marshall, 'On some of the water birds frequenting Belfast Lough' *Dubin Penny Journal* 3 1834 pp 18-19 and in an article in the Belfast News-Letter April 2 1983 p. 4; Evidence that the present large rookery at Belvoir is long established is suggested by the name Corbie Wood for the area towards the river, corbie being a Scottish word for a rook or crow. Also a notice in the Belfast News-Letter of 24 May 1768 p. 2 describes an extraordinary all day crow shoot at Newforge, an event that suggests that there was large crow population in the area.

30 Thomas T. Kelly, *A history of Holywood* (Belfast, 1850), pp 67-68.

31 J. Drummond 'Notes on Belfast Botanic Garden and a few country seats in the counties Down and Antrim, Ireland' *The Scottish gardener* 3 (1854), pp 207-211, 341-345, 379-384.

32 Advertisements in Belfast News-Letter 21 May 1799 p. 3; 10 March 1809 p. 3.

33 Article in the Belfast News-Letter 25 October 1831 p. 2. The trees William Pirrie planted most likely formed the wood shown on the first edition (1834) 6 inch map sheet 6 just southwest of Conlig.

34 Advertisement in Belfast News-Letter 3 February 1843 p. 3. The impressive scale of the planting undertaken around this period can be seen from the 1st revision 6 inch map (sheet 1, 1858).

35 Peter Rankin, 'Clandeboye house' in Anon, *Clandeboye* Ulster Architectural Heritage Society (Belfast, 1985), pp 26-27.

36 Clandeboye papers PRONI See for example D/1071/A/K/1C/11/1.

37 Lord Dufferin's instructions to Mr Thompson. November 1861. PRONI D/1071/A/K/1B/10/1.

38 Personal observation, 2008

39 Dufferin correspondence. Letter dated 7 January 1887, Letter dated 25 September 1887. PRONI D/1071/A/K/1C/11/1.

40 Advertisements in Belfast News-Letter 2 February 1770 p. 3; See Appendix 3.

41 Advertisement in Belfast News-Letter 29 January 1830 p. 3.

42 Samuel M'Skimin, The *history and antiquities of the county of the town of Carrickfergus* (Belfast, 1811), pp 116, 120.

43 For example advertisements for the sales of 'thinnings of plantations' at Whitehouse, Northern Whig 6 April 1847 p. 3 and '103 lots of light timber' at Clandeboye, Northern Whig 27 November 1849 p. 3. Examples of trees felled for timber include sale of 400 trees at Bell-Mount and Cabin-Hill, Belfast News-Letter 12 March 1841 p. 3 and a sale at Belvoir, Northern Whig 28 January 1851 p. 3.

44 Although it has been stated that the larger trees at Ormeau were felled around the 1860s (W. A. Maguire, 'Ormeau House' *Ulster Journal of Archaeology* 42 (1979), pp 66-71), today there are several trees at Ormeau with a girth of 4m or greater which must predate the formation of the park. Also at the opening of the park the site was described as being 'remarkably well wooded' News-Letter 17 April 1871 p. 3.

45 James Fraser, *Handbook for travellers in Ireland* (Dublin, 1859), p. 181.

46 Dufferin papers. Letter of 25 September 1887 PRONI D/1071/A/K/1C/11/1; letter of 5 April 1865 D/1071/A/K/1B/14/1.

47 Article in Belfast News-Letter 15 January 1839 p. 1.

48 Anon, *Report of the departmental committee on Irish forestry* Department of agriculture and technical instruction for Ireland (Dublin, 1908), p. 198. This was probably the storm of 21-22 December 1894, see article in Belfast Telegraph 22 January 1946 p. 2.

49 Samuel M'Skimin, The *history and antiquities of the county of the town of Carrickfergus* (Belfast, 1811), pp 112, 121, 127.

50 Angélique Day and Patrick McWilliams, *Ordnance Survey memoirs of Ireland. Parishes of County Antrim XIV 1832, 1839-40 Volume 37* Institute of Irish studies (Belfast, 1990), pp 8, 159.

51 Angélique Day and Patrick McWilliams, *Ordnance Survey memoirs of Ireland. Parishes of County Antrim I 1838-9 Volume 2* Institute of Irish studies (Belfast, 1990), p. 37

52 Personal observation.

53 George Benn, *The History of the Town of Belfast* (Belfast, 1823), pp 179-180.

54 Ralph Tate, *Flora Belfastiensis* (Belfast, 1863), p. 54.

55 Anon, *Report of the departmental committee on Irish forestry* Department of agriculture and technical instruction for Ireland (Dublin, 1908), p. 198.

56 Advertisement in Belfast News-Letter 23 August 1811 p. 3. See also advertisement for the sale of Lisnabreene, Belfast News-Letter 24 May 1836 p. 3 and Appendix 3.

57 See Appendix 3.

58 Anon, 'Excursion to Mr. Valentine's fernery and the Duncrue salt mines' *Annual report of the Belfast Naturalists' Field Club* 5 (1868) pp 10-13.

59   William Laffan (ed.), *Painting Ireland. Topographical views from Glin Castle* (Tralee, 2006) pp 135-136.

60   Article in Belfast News-Letter 7 June 1875 p. 3; Anon, 'Woodburn' *Annual Report and Proceedings of the Belfast Naturalists' Field Club* Series 2, 2 (1885) pp 413-415. The path is unfortunately now in poor condition. A wooden flight of steps have decayed and the path is in places covered in rubble and mud, elsewhere eroded by the stream. It is not open to the public.

61   W. A. Maguire, 'Lords and landlords – the Donegall family' in J. C. Beckett et al, *Belfast. The making of the city* (Belfast, 1988), pp 27-39.

62   Advertisement in Belfast News-Letter 20 September 1825 p. 3 refers to the Deer Park and land by the Throne and Ormeau as being Donegall's 'particular preserve'; A park keeper at Cave Hill is referred to in documents of 1837 relating to a dispute about limestone quarries in the area (PRONI D/2930/3/15/1-31). David Symes was reported in 1845 to have been 'late of the Deer-Park, and for 40 years Gamekeeper to the Marquis of Donegall' Northern Whig 1 November 1845 p. 3.

63   William Thompson, *The natural history of Ireland* volume 3 (London, 1851), p. 277 notes that in October 1833 he had seen a fallow deer that had been killed by its companions in the park at Cave Hill and added a comment from the gamekeeper about the deer in the park.

64   Correspondence: Lord Donegall to T Verner. PRONI D/1798/7/24, 28, 30, 31, 33 (Letter 24 was missing, transcript used). It is highly likely that the deer referred to in these letters were in the Cave Hill Deer Park, though the location is not mentioned. It is puzzling that none of the many descriptions of Cave Hill by Victorian travel writers that have been examined mention the deer park or deer. Notes of 1837 for a legal dispute about quarrying on Cave Hill (PRONI D/2930/3/15/1-31) also make no reference to deer but do mention ploughing and crops of corn. Perhaps at times there were no deer or they were kept corralled?

65   Correspondence: Lord Donegall to T Verner. PRONI D/1798/12/17.

66   Advertisements for sale of deer herd placed in Belfast News-Letter 1 January 1859 p. 2, 20 January 1859 p. 2.

67   Note in Belfast News-Letter 22 November 1864 p. 2; Contract to build the Castle was advertised in the News-Letter on 11 April 1868 p. 1; In July 1871 the Castle was 'rapidly approaching completion' *Annual Report of the Belfast Field Naturalists' Club* 9 (1872) pp 11-13.

68   Donegall Estate Cash Account from 1 January till 30 June 1870. Expenditure for January 15 1870. PRONI D/853/13/5; A visit to the Deer Park in 1871, described in the *Annual Report of the Belfast Field Naturalists' Club* 9 (1872) pp 11-13, referred to trees that had been recently planted but unfortunately gave no more details.

69   Donegall estate cash account 1 January to 30 June 1870. Income from the sale of 468 rabbits killed in the deer park on 29 January 1870. PRONI D/835/13/5; Pheasant are mentioned in the Belfast News-Letter 29 October 1873 p. 3.

70   In 2007, two fallen Scots pine trees from near the main path to Cave Hill, at a conifer plantation near the top of the woodland (332780 379720) were sampled. These trees (ref Q10873, Q10874) had start dates of 1896 and 1904. A third Scots pine tree (Q10875) which was sampled from high up the stem gave a date of 1916. This is not thought to reflect the planting date and so has been omitted from the study. The planting date of the large girthed conifers growing by the Castle is not known but as early (c.1900) postcards of the castle shows conifers as saplings, it seems likely that they were all planted around this period.

71   The Countess of Shaftsbury Cash Book. PRONI D/835/12/1.

Chapter 6. Trees and parks for the people

1   Letter in the Belfast News-Letter 3 July 1827 p. 1. See also reply in the Belfast News-Letter 6 July 1827 p. 2.

2   Article in Northern Whig 1 September 1825 p. 4.

3   An advertisement for the 'Royal Pleasure Gardens' with entrances from Fredrick Street and York Lane appeared around the time of the visit by Queen Victoria, see the Northern Whig 9 August 1849 p. 3; The 'Belfast Borough Park' on the Antrim Road was mentioned as a venue for foot races. See the Belfast News-Letter 3 April 1863 p. 3, 7 April 1863 p. 3, 5 May 1863 p. 3 and advertisement for races held on 11 and 13 July 1863.

4   Article in Belfast News-Letter 1 June 1827 p. 1.

5   Note in Northern Whig 10 January 1828 p. 13 and 18 May 1829 p. 3. The history of the site is mentioned in Anon, *A popular guide to the Royal Botanic Garden of Belfast* (Belfast, 1851) pp viii – ix; The setting is briefly mentioned by James Thomson, *On public parks in connexion*

with large towns with a suggestion for the formation of a park in Belfast (Belfast, 1852); See also The most Hon. George Augustus Marquis of Donegall to John McCance, Wm. Tennant, Valentine Whitla Esq. trustees of the Botanic Society. Lease for 999 years from Nov. 1828. PRONI D/811/422/1.

6   Anon, 'Belfast Botanic and Horticultural Society' *The Gardener's Magazine* 4 (1828) pp 164-165; Article in the Belfast News-Letter 11 March 1828 p. 2.

7   Article in Northern Whig 10 January 1828 p. 13.

8   Article in Northern Whig 17 May 1838 p. 2.

9   The Coronation fete is described in the Northern Whig 30 June 1838 p. 2. For advertisement seeking apprentices see Belfast News-Letter on 12 February 1839 p. 3. The adoption of a plan for the erection of a glass house is noted in the Belfast News-Letter 14 May 1839 p. 2. For further details see Eileen McCracken, *The Palm House and Botanic Garden, Belfast* Ulster Architectural Heritage Society (Belfast, 1971).

10   Report of the committee of the Belfast Botanic Society, Northern Whig 24 May 1830 p. 4; Annual meeting of the Belfast Botanical and Horticultural Society, Belfast News-Letter 16 June 1837 p. 4.

11   Anon, *A popular guide to the Botanic Garden of Belfast* (Belfast, 1851).

12   Anon, 'Royal Belfast Botanic Garden' *The Farmer's Gazette* 3 (1845) pp 732-733; J. Drummond, 'Notes on Belfast Botanic Garden and a few country seats in the counties Down and Antrim, Ireland' *The Scottish gardener* 3 (1854) pp 207-211, 341-345, 379-384.

13   Northern Whig 2 June 1840 p. 2 and 11 May 1848 p. 2.

14   Anon, 'Walks for the working classes' *The Belfast People's Magazine* 1 (1848) pp 167-169; Anon, The Working Classes' Association and the Botanic Garden *The Belfast People's Magazine* 1 (1848) pp 215-216.

15   Articles in Belfast News-Letter 6 May 1865 p. 2, 3.

16   Articles in Northern Whig 31 July 1851 p. 2; Belfast News-Letter 11 April 1855 p. 2, 19 April 1870 p. 3, 30 March 1875 p. 3.

17   Meeting of the Royal Belfast Botanic and Horticultural Company, Belfast News-Letter 18 May 1892 p. 3.

18   Meeting of the Royal Belfast Botanic and Horticultural Company, Belfast News-Letter 12 January 1893 p. 7.

19   Meeting of the Royal Belfast Botanic and Horticultural Company, Belfast News-Letter 20 March 1894 p. 6.

20   Eileen Black, *The People's Park* (Belfast, 1988); Belfast News-Letter 13 August 1850 pp 1-2.

21   See discussion in Northern Whig 18 February 1851 p. 2, Belfast News-Letter 5 February 1851 p. 2, 19 February 1851 p. 2; Advertisement seeking proposals Northern Whig 26 April 1851 p. 3; Inauguration of building Northern Whig 6 September 1851 p. 2.

22   Articles in Northern Whig 29 July 1851 p. 2, 6 September 1851 p. 2, 23 September 1851 p. 2.

23   Articles in Belfast News-Letter 19 February 1851 p. 2, 28 March 1851 p. 2.

24   Eileen Black, *The People's Park* (Belfast, 1988).

25   Article in Belfast News-Letter 4 April 1863 p. 3.

26   Articles in Belfast News-Letter 2 April 1861 p. 3, 7 April 1863 p. 3.

27   Eileen Black, *The People's Park* (Belfast, 1988).

28   James Thomson, *On parks in connexion with large towns with a suggestion for the formation of a park in Belfast* (Belfast, 1852).

29   W. M. O'Hanlon, *Walks among the poor of Belfast and suggestions for their improvement* (Belfast, 1853), pp 83-88.

30   W. M. O'Hanlon, *Walks among the poor of Belfast and suggestions for their improvement* (Belfast, 1853), pp 22-23.

31   Articles in Belfast News-Letter 13 August 1855 p 2; 20 August 1855 p. 2.

32   Information about the Association can be found in a book of cuttings, PRONI D/410/7. The rules of the association are given in Anon, *The Association for the protection of public rights of way in an around Belfast* (Belfast, 1856). The right of way court case is described in Anon, *Report of the trial of the indictment. The Queen v. Magill, tried at the County of Antrim summer assizes, 1859, (held at Belfast) before the Lord Chiel Baron Pigot* (Belfast, 1859) for details regarding the Cave Hill case. A copy of these two publications was kindly lent by Mr Adam Brett in 2007.

33   Robert Scott, *A breath of fresh air. The story of Belfast's parks* (Belfast, 2000), p. 48.

34   Article in Belfast News-Letter 3 November 1855 p. 1.

35   Article in Belfast News-Letter 29 May 1863 pp 2-3; See discussion about Victoria Park in the Harbour Commissioners Annual Meeting, Belfast News-Letter 29 January 1864.

36   Article in Northern Whig 8 February 1865 p. 3.

37   Earl of Shaftsbury Estate. Cost Book 1862-1889. Meeting of 16 July 1864. p. 18 PRONI D/835/11/1

38 Robert Scott, *A breath of fresh air. The story of Belfast's parks* (Belfast, 2000), pp 9-10; The Parks Sub-Committee first met on 12 October 1865. For this and other early minutes see Miscellaneous Committee Minute Books 1859-1869 PRONI LA/7/16AB/3/2.

39 Two maps showing proposed housing lots at Ormeau were produced in 1865 (PRONI D/971/M1/3). An advertisement to let the demesne at Ormeau for housing was placed in the Belfast News-Letter on 15 October 1867 p. 1. The first notice about the plan to build a new mansion in the Deer Park dates from 1864. See section on Cave Hill in previous chapter.

40 The 'Act to afford facilities for the Establishment and Maintenance of Public Parks in Ireland' is described in the Belfast News-Letter 20 July 1869 p. 4; Robert Scott, *A breath of fresh air. The story of Belfast's parks* (Belfast, 2000) p. 14. For decision to acquire land see Special Meeting of Council 1 November 1869, Minute book of the Town Council PRONI LA/7/2EA/9 pp 156-159.

41 Meeting of Belfast Town Council reported in the Belfast News-Letter 2 May 1872 p. 4.

42 Meeting of the Parks Committee 10 October 1872 Minute book of the Parks Committee PRONI LA/7/11AA/1 p. 3-6; Discussions about the submissions can be found in the meetings of Belfast Town Council, see reports in Belfast News-Letter on 2 November 1872 p. 3, 3 December 1872 p. 3, 3 January 1873 p. 4, 9 June 1873 p. 4; Correspondence in the Belfast News-Letter 11 June 1873 p. 4, 12 June p. 4, 13 June p. 3, 14 June p. 4.

43 Meeting of Belfast Town Council reported in Belfast News-Letter 17 June 1873 p. 4.

44 Meeting of Belfast Town Council reported in Belfast News-Letter 9 September 1873 p. 4; Advertisement in the Belfast News-Letter 9 January 1874 p. 2.

45 The early development of Ormeau is described in an article in the Belfast News Letter 1 July 1875 p. 3; Minute book of the Parks Committee. PRONI LA/7/11AA/1 p. 83.

46 Minute book of the Parks Committee Meeting of 10 March 1879 (Mr Mann), Meeting of 12 October 1881(rhododendron). PRONI LA/7/11AA/1 pp 265, 352.

47 Minute book of the Parks Committee Meeting of 10 April 1878 (deer from the earl of Antrim), Meeting of 25 October 1881 (emu donated by Henry Campbell of Lorne, Craigavad). PRONI LA/7/11AA/1 pp 233, 353.

48 Minute book of Town Council Special meeting of Council 1 November 1869, 1 January 1870, 22 April 1871. LA/7/2EA/9. pp 156-9, 225, 624; Article in Northern Whig 21 May 1872 p. 3.

49 Minute book of the Parks Committee. Meetings of the 1 March 1879 and 16 January 1884. PRONI LA/7/11AA/1 pp 263, 420.

50 Robert Scott, *A breath of fresh air. The story of Belfast's parks* (Belfast, 2000) pp 21, 23, 24, 26, 37, 50.

51 Minute book of the Town Improvement Committee. Meeting of 19 June 1872, 15 April 1874, 16 February 1876 PRONI LA/7/20AA/4 pp 47, 48, 306, 577.

52 Minute book of the Town Improvement Committee. Meeting of 31 March 1886 (Clifton Street), 25 May 1887 (Crumlin Road), 2 November 1887 (Botanic). PRONI LA/7/20AA/7 pp 171, 332, 394.

53 Minute book of the Town Improvement Committee. Meeting of 14 October 1885. PRONI LA/7/20AA/7 p. 119.

54 Minute book of the Town Improvement Committee. Meeting of 12 February 1896. PRONI LA/7/20AA/9 p. 549.

55 Minute book of the Parks Committee. Meeting of 24 February 1889. PRONI LA/7/11AA/1 p. 574

56 Minute book of the Town Improvement Committee. Meeting of 17 November 1886. PRONI LA/7/20AA/7 p. 244.

57 Minute book of the Town Improvement Committee. Meeting of 4 December 1900. PRONI LA/7/20AA/12 p. 76.

Chapter 7. Decades of neglect

1 Anon, *Report of the departmental committee on Irish forestry* HMSO (Dublin, 1908).

2 Emrys Jones, *A social geography of Belfast* (London, 1960), p. 66.

3 Articles in Belfast Evening Telegraph 29 September 1905 p. 6, 18 April 1906 p. 3 and 8 June 1907 p. 6.

4 Article in Belfast Evening Telegraph 28 September 1905 p. 2, 4 April 1906 p. 6; Advertisement in Belfast Evening Telegraph 13 April 1906 p. 3; Anon, 'The garden city in Belfast' *The Irish builder and engineer* 5 May (1906) pp 360-363

5 C. E. B. Brett, *Buildings of Belfast 1700-1914* revised edition (Belfast, 1985) p. 73. See also the paper by Joseph McConnell on garden

suburbs delivered to the Auctioneers' Institute session 1910-1911. Copy in PRONI D/2964/XA/7

6 Personal observation.

7 Article in The Northern Whig 18 April 1910 p. 9.

8 Reginald George McCaddan, *The Wilson Story* (Belfast, 1978).

9 Letter in the Belfast Evening Telegraph 16 May 1906 p. 2; Minute book of the Town Improvement Committee 1900-1902. Meetings of 25 June and 9 July 1901 (Parkmount Avenue) LA/7/20AA/12 pp 238, 248. Minute book of the Town Improvement Committee 1907-1909. Meetings of 13 and 15 October 1908. (Miss Mary Thompson) PRONI LA/7/20AA/16 pp 554, 556.

10 Minute book of the Town Improvement Committee 1909-1910 Meeting 12 October 1909. (Wellington Park) PRONI LA/7/20AA/17 p. 328.

11 Hugh Shearman, *Ulster* (London, 1949), p. 189.

12 Personal observation. Information provided by Mr Rutherford, Stranmillis College in 2007.

13 Anon, *Clandeboye* Ulster Architectural Heritage Society (Belfast, 1985), p. 41

14 Ben Simon (ed.), *A treasured landscape. The heritage of Belvoir Park* (Belfast, 2005) Chapter 2.

15 Article in Belfast Telegraph 13 November 1933 p. 10.

16 Robert Scott, *A breath of fresh air. The story of Belfast's parks* (Belfast, 2000), p. 95; Article in Irish Times 29 January 1934 p. 8.

17 Brian McNeill, *Stormont Estate. Woodland and management report.* Prepared by Estate and Forestry Services for Department of the Environment NI. 3 volumes (Belfast, 1987).

18 C. S. Kilpatrick, *Northern Ireland Forest Service. A history* Department of Agriculture NI (Belfast, 1988), p. 35.

19 Nóirín Dobson, *Colin Glen a history* Lisburn Peace and Reconciliation Project for Colin Glen Trust (Belfast, 2000), p. 42.

20 The date when this woodland on Collin Mountain was felled is not known, though it is shown on the 1 inch map of 1936 and is absent on the 1951 map.

21 Brian McNeill, *Stormont Estate. Woodland and management report.* 3 volumes Prepared by Estate and Forestry Services for Department of the Environment NI (Belfast, 1987); George Beale and Eamon Phoenix, *Stran. Stranmillis College 1922-1998* (Belfast, 1998), p. 114.

22 Note in Belfast News-Letter 21 December 1940.

23 Information from Clarke Cunningham, Killyleagh in 2008; Meeting of the Improvement Committee, 2 March, 3 August, 31 August 1943. Minutes of the Improvement Committee. PRONI LA/7/20AA/33 pp 86, 102, 105.

24 Lyn Gallagher and Dick Rodgers, *Castle, coast and cottage* (Belfast, 1986), pp 121-122; see also article in Belfast Telegraph 15 June 1946 p. 2, 3 January 1963 p. 2. A third area of woodland near Belfast, Cregagh Glen at Lisnabreeny, was an even earlier acquisition for the Trust (in 1938). It had been gifted and was not subject to a fund raising campaign.

25 For the Belfast Civic Society records see PRONI D/3760/2/2.

26 Anon, *Planning proposals for the Belfast area. Interim report of the Planning Commission* Cmd 227 HMSO (Belfast, 1945).

27 Anon, *The Ulster Countryside. Interim report of the Northern Ireland Planning Advisory Board* HMSO (Belfast, 1946).

28 The constitution is given in Central Gardens Association publication *The Ulster Garden Handbook for 1957* (Belfast, 1957). The best kept village and town competition is described in the *Ulster Garden Handbook 1967* pp 65-67.

29 Wilfrid Capper, *Caring for the countryside A history of 50 years of the Ulster Society for the Preservation of the Countryside* (Belfast, 1988), pp 22-27.

30 Information from Robert Carson, landscape architect, in 2008; Robert Carson, *Landscape aspects of road design.* Ministry of Development HMSO (Belfast, 1969).

31 Information provided by Brian Woods, landscape architect, in 2008.

32 P. J. Newbould, 'Conservation' in R. H. Buchanan and B. M. Walker, (eds) *Province, city and People. Belfast and its region* (Antrim, 1987), pp 79-98.

33 Central Gardens Association, *Ulster Garden Handbook 1967* (Belfast, 1967), pp 62-63. Article in Belfast Telegraph 7 November 1967 p. 7.

34 Information provided by Robert Carson, Landscape Architect, in 2008. Robert also kindly showed me a booklet *Horticultural Planning in the urban landscape* comprising papers given at a conference at Greenmount College on 15 March 1967 and printed for HMSO by Century Newspapers. This was organized by the Horticultural Division of the NI Ministry of Agriculture which the forward of the booklet stated was one of five conferences held on landscaping, including roadside and motorway planting, urban planting and the industrial landscape.

35 C. S. Kilpatrick, *Northern Ireland Forest Service. A history* (Belfast, 1987), pp 52, 55, 58.
36 Robert H. Mathew, *Belfast Regional Survey and Plan 1962* HMSO (Belfast, 1964).
37 Building Design Partnership, *Belfast Urban Area Plan*. Two volumes (London, 1969).
38 Anon, 'The protection of trees' *Ulster Garden Handbook* (1974) p. 91; Information about the Wesley Tree provided by Planning Service. Comments on the implementation of TPO legislation are from personal experience.
39 Information from the Northern Ireland Environment Agency.
40 Alf McCreary, *Making a difference. The story of Ulster Garden Villages Ltd* (Belfast, 1999); Information kindly provided by Ulster Garden Villages in 2008.
41 Information from former Parks staff, 2008.
42 Article in the Belfast Telegraph 9 January 1964 p. 5; The importance of tree planting for the city area was also highlighted in a document by Building Design Partnership, *A report to Belfast Corporation on planning policy in the city centre* (Belfast, 1969), p. 65, but again this recommendation was not implemented.
43 Robert Scott, *A breath of fresh air. The story of Belfast's parks* (Belfast, 2000).
44 Anon, *Northern Ireland Agriculture, 24 General Report of the Ministry of Agriculture. Year ended 31 March 1965* HMSO Cmd 486 (Belfast, 1965), pp 94-95; Brian McNeill, *Stormont Estate. Woodland and management report*. 3 volumes Prepared by Estate and Forestry Services for Department of the Environment NI (Belfast, 1987).
45 Anon, *Northern Ireland Agriculture, 27 General Report of the Ministry of Agriculture. Year ended 31 March 1968* HMSO Cmd 523 (Belfast, 1968), p. 98; Anon, 'A new deal for private forestry in Northern Ireland' *Irish Forestry* 25 (1968) pp 52-53.
46 Personal observation; One such conifer planting project involved 2-3,000 trees being supplied to the Lagan Valley Regional Pak for the higher ground around the Lagan Meadows. Information from LVRP Committee minutes of 19 March and 28 May 1976.
47 Information provided by Cecil Kilpatrick, former head of Forest Service in 2007.
48 Ben Simon (ed.), *A treasured landscape. The heritage of Belvoir Park.* (Belfast, 2005) Chapter 2.
49 Information from Forest Service files; Government of Northern Ireland, *Statement by the Minister of Agriculture for Northern Ireland prepared for the British Commonwealth Forestry Conference 1957* HMSO (Belfast, 1956).
50 Information provided by Cecil Kilpatrick, former head of Forest Service in 2007 and by Brian Woods, landscape architect, in 2008.

Chapter 8. The second great tree planting project

1   Information provided by staff of Belfast Parks and Cemeteries Services in 2007.
2   Parks Department files.
3   Article in the Belfast Telegraph 13 May 1985 p. 9.
4   Information provided by staff of Belfast Parks and Cemeteries Services in 2007.
5   Belfast Parks files, information from Maurice Parkinson, former Head of Parks in 2006.
6   Information provided by former staff of Belfast Parks and Cemeteries Services including Margaret Lindsay, Raymond Harrison and Maurice Parkinson, Former Head of Parks in 2006.
7   Belfast Parks files.
8   Belfast Parks files.
9   Information provided by Sean Minshull, Landscape Architect, Belfast Parks and Cemeteries Services in 2008.
10 Information provided by Dougie Elliott former Assistant Area Manager, Belfast Parks and Cemeteries Services in 2006.
11 Information provided by Reg Maxwell Area Manager and Fiona Holdsworth Principal Parks and Cemeteries Services Manager, Belfast City Council in 2007.
12 Information provided by Craig Wallace, former Director of Parks in 2007; Article in Belfast Newsletter 22 March 1984 p. 3.
13 Article in the Belfast Telegraph 6 October 1984 p. 1.
14 Article in the Belfast Telegraph 13 May 1985 p. 9; Information provided by Alan McHaffie, Woodland/Recreation Manager, Belfast Parks and Cemeteries Services in 2006.
15 Department of the Environment (NI), Belfast Urban Area Plan 2001 (Belfast, 1990) p. 49.
16 Information provided by Alan McHaffie, Woodland/Recreation

Manager, Belfast Parks and Cemeteries Services in 2006.
17 Personal observation.
18 Information provided in 2008 by Pat Craig, formerly with the Housing Executive and now Operations Director of the Woodland Trust in Northern Ireland, and Robert Carson, Landscape Architect.
19 Information provided in 2008 by Pat Craig, formerly with the Housing Executive and now Operations Director of the Woodland Trust in Northern Ireland.
20 Information provided by the Housing Executive staff and personal observation.
21 Article in Sunday News 18 December 1977 p. 7.
22 J. Craig Wallace, 'Towards a brighter Belfast' *Ulster Garden Handbook* (1974) pp 71-73; Article in Belfast Telegraph 21 January 1981 p. 10.
23 Parks files; Article in Belfast Telegraph 21 January 1981 p. 10.
24 Personal observation; Information provided by Paul Barr, Landscape Planning and Development Manager, Belfast Parks and Cemeteries Services in 2007.
25 Article in Belfast Telegraph 21 January 1981 p. 10; Information provided by staff involved in urban regeneration and Paul Barr, Landscape Planning and Development Manager, Belfast Parks and Cemeteries Services in 2007.
26 Personal observation.
27 Peter Hunter and Roy A. Adams, *Laganside* BDP Design (Belfast, 1987).
28 'Laganlife' leaflet produced by Laganside Corporation with the Ulster Wildlife Trust in the 1980s; Personal involvement.
29 Personal observation; Information provided by Neil Rainey, Landscape Architect in 2007. Unfortunately they were removed during road works in 2008.
30 Information provided by Philip Blackstock, forestry consultant, in 2007.
31 Information provided in 2008 by Sue Christie, formerly head of UWT and now Director of Northern Ireland Environment Link and Mike Meharg, one of the founder members of CVNI and now Head of Biodiversity Unit, Northern Ireland Environment Agency.
32 Belfast parks files.
33 Article in the Sunday News 3 July 1977 p. 8.
34 C. S. Kilpatrick, *Northern Ireland Forest Service. A history* Department of Agriculture NI (Belfast, 1988), pp 80-82.
35 Article in the Belfast Newsletter 18 May 1973 p. 9
36 Personal observation; Information provided by Sue Christie, formerly Director of UWT and currently Director of Northern Ireland Environment Link in 2008.
37 Department of the Environment (NI), Belfast Urban Area Plan 2001 (Belfast, 1990) p. 50.
38 Mark Johnston, 'The Forest of Belfast: healing the environment and the community' *Arboricultural Journal* 19 (1995) pp 53-72; Ben Simon, 'Tree traditions and folklore from northeast Ireland' *Arboricultural Journal* 24 (2000) 15-40; Ben Simon, 'The Forest of Belfast – a growing success' in Kevin D. Collins (ed.) *Proceedings of Ireland's third National conference on urban forestry*. Tree Council of Ireland (Dublin, 1999), pp 11-15; Ben Simon, *Carving a future for Belfast* (Belfast, 2006).
39 Alicia Segoviano, *Belfast's Trees. A survey of trees in Greater Belfast*. A report by Forest of Belfast (Belfast, 1995).
40 Information provided by Robert Scott, Conservation and Promotion Manager, Belfast Parks and Cemeteries Services in 2008.
41 Information provided by education staff involved in these organizations.
42 Information provided by Ian Humphreys, formerly Education Officer with CVNI, now Chief Executive of Tidy NI in 2007; Dinah Browne, (ed.) *Our Trees. A guide to growing Northern Ireland's native trees from seed*. Conservation Volunteers (Belfast, 1996).
43 Information provided by Tim Duffy, Chief Executive of the Colin Glen Trust; Noirin Dobson, *Colin Glen. A history*. Lisburn Peace and Reconciliation Project (Belfast, 2000); Article in Belfast Telegraph 10 January 1989 p. 9.
44 Information provided by staff at Belfast Parks and Cemeteries Services in 2007.
45 Information provided by people involved in these schemes including Pat Cregg, Operations Director in Northern Ireland.
46 Personal involvement; Information provided by Ian Humphreys, formerly Education Officer with CVNI, now Chief Executive of Tidy NI in 2007.

Chapter 9. The future of the urban forest

1. Elm were particularly common at Big Wood in Belvoir Park, Hydebank (where 70-80 tall elms had to be felled), Cregagh Glen, in the north eastern part of the Stormont estate and at Belfast Castle Estate. There was a good collection of elms at the Botanic Gardens. There were some elm street trees, but it was not commonly planted on pavements. Following the first evidence of Dutch elm disease at Barnett demesne, a report of 1987 noted that some of the elms at Belfast Castle were infected and at Stormont in the same year symptoms of the disease were noted in woodland in the central part of the estate. In the following years, all the mature elms in these woods died. Information provided by Fiona Holdsworth, Principal Parks and Cemetery Services Operation Manager, Reg Maxwell, Area Manager, Belfast Parks, Mark Parker of Forest Service, in the report by Brian McNeill, *Stormont Estate. Woodland and management report*. Prepared by Estate and Forestry Services for Department of the Environment NI 3 volumes (Belfast, 1987). A few isolated large elms have survived in the urban area, noted by the author in graveyards (one at Friar's Bush and Clifton Street) and in boundary plantings (eg one at Inst. and one at the Theological College).

2. Article in the Belfast Telegraph 14 January 1953 p. 4; Robert Scott, *Wild Belfast on safari in the city* (Belfast, 2004) pp 36-37; Personal observation.

3. Anon, *Forestry in Northern Ireland. Consultation paper*. Department of Agriculture and Rural Development (Belfast, 2002).

Holy Trinity Church, Drumbo

Appendix 1

References to wood rangers in surviving 18th century Donegall Estate accounts.
Taken from records in PRONI T/3425/3/9-18.

1733. Benjamin Singleton [?] received £3 for one year and a half salary for a wood ranger 'in the Fall'.

1734. William Brown received £6 for one year's salary as wood ranger.

1734. Brien Carr received £2 for a year's salary 'as wood ranger in the Fall, Mallone and Dunmurry'.

1735. William Brown received £6 for a year's wages as wood ranger.

1735. Brien Carr received £2 for a year's salary as wood ranger in the Fall, Mallone and Dunmurry.

1736. William Brown received £6 for one year's salary as wood ranger.

1736. Borckey [?] McCliney received £2 for one year's salary 'as wood ranger of the Fall, Mallone and Dunmurry'.

1737. William Browne received £6 for one year's salary as wood ranger.

1737. Edward Fisher received £1 'for half a year's salary for taking care of his Lordships Timber in the Fall Mallone Dunmurry'.

1738. William Brown received £3 for a half year's salary as wood ranger.

1738. Edward Fisher received £1 for half a year's salary 'as wood ranger to his Lordship'

1738. Edward Fisher received £1 'for half a year's salary due me for taking care of said Earls hedge roes in the Fall & Mallone ....'

1739. William Brown received £3 for a half year's salary 'for taking care of his Lordship's wood at Belfast called Crumock.'

1739. Edward Fisher received £2 for one year's salary 'due me as Wood Ranger of the Fall'

1740. Edward Fisher received £1 for half a year's salary as 'Ranger of his Lordships Woods in the Fall.'

1740. William Brown received £6 for one year's salary 'as Ranger of Crumoak Wood.'

1740. Esther Fisher received £1 10s for 'three quarters salary due my husband…as Woodranger of the Fall.'

1741. William Brown received £6 for one year's salary 'as ranger of Crumock Wood'

1741. William Brown received £3 for half a year's salary …'as woodranger of Cromack.'

1741. John Woods received £1 for half a year's salary as 'woodranger of the Fall'.

1742. John Woods received £1 for half a year's salary as 'woodranger in the Fall'.

1742. John Woods received £1 for half a year's salary as 'ranger of the Fall woods'.

1742. William Brown received £3 for half a year's salary 'as ranger of Crumoak Wood.'

1742. William Brown received £3 for half a year's salary 'as ranger of Crumoak Wood.'

1743. William Brown received £3 for half a year's salary as 'wood ranger of Crumoak'

Appendix 2

Advertisements for tree sales in the Belfast area noted in early issues of the News-Letter

Sale at Drumbeg, 6 April 1739. 'a Quantity of Timber fit for Coopers, building Country Houses or other Uses'.

Sale at Drumbeg Demesne, 22 March 1757. 'a large Quantity of Timber, consisting of Fir and Ash, the Fir of both large and small Scantling [size], fit for Deals, Pipes, Ladders, or Building; the Ash for Hoops, Splitts, Cars, Plows, etc'.

Sale at Holywood House, 26 October 1759. 'a quantity of good Alder timber.'

Sale at Ballymeckan near Holywood, 18 November 1766. 'a Variety of large Ash, Sycamore and Elm Trees'.

Sale at Purdy's-burn, 6 March 1767. 'a large Quantity of Ash Timber. Also some Sycamore Trees fit for Beams etc.'

Sale at Cultra House, 1 November 1768. 'some Ash, Beech, Sycamore, Alder and Fir Timber'.

Sale at Stranmillis, 12 February 1771. 'For COOPERS…to be sold to the highest bidder…two ozier gardens, situate at Stranmillis near the Malone Turnpike.'

Sale at Mount Pottinger [Ballymacarret], 16 July 1771. 'a Number of Full-grown Fir Trees in prime Condition, very fit for Pipes or any other Purpose that Fir Timber is generally made use of.'

Sale at Bangor, 11 August 1772. 'several Fir Trees in the Grove of Bangor'.

Sale at Drum [Drumbeg], 16 October 1772. 'a Number of fine Ash Trees: also some remarkable large Walnut'.

Sale at Belvoir Park, 4 December 1772. 'between twenty and thirty Elm and Ash Trees, some of them large.'

Sale at Bangor, 12 March 1773. 'some very fine large full grown Ash; as also some middling sized Sycamore, and some Firr Trees.'

Sale at Holywood House, 4-8 November 1774. 'a considerable Quantity of Ash Timber fit for Cars, Ploughs and Harrows, and some Irish Fir and Poplar'.

Sale at Belvoir Park, 10 December 1783. 'a quantity of ash and other timber…fit for various uses in husbandry'

Sale at Holywood Demesne, 23-27 January 1797. 'Nearly Two Hundred ASH TREES, a Quantity of which will be fit for Broad Hoops and Riddle Splits together with a number of Poplar, Fir and Alder Trees'.

Sale at Belvoir Park, 10 January 1800. 'Several Hundreds of Oak, Ash, Elm and Beech Trees…in the Wood between Newtownbreda and Purdysburn – the above will be well worth the attention of Bleachers, Farmers, Ship-builders, Coach-makers, Mill and Wheel Wrights, Coopers, Carpenters, etc'.

Sale at Ballybeen, Dundonald, 24 January 1804. 'A LARGE quantity of remarkably fine Ash Timber'.

Sale at Belvoir Park, 18 April 1809. 'several Thousands of NICE YOUNG POLES, chiefly Larch with some Ash, Scotch Fir, Beech etc. From 12 to 40 Feet in Length… Also many Thousands of FAGGOTS, made from the Branches of those Trees'.

Sale at Belvoir Park, 10 April 1810. 'A CONSIDERABLE Quantity of very Fine Full-aged OAK TREES….The Purchaser may take his own time for Cutting, for the better preservation of the Bark.'

Appendix 3

Records of tree planting registered by tenants for the Belfast region

Date and page in Dublin Gazette		Person registering trees	Location	Parish	Number of trees
1790	p. 636	John Hancock	Lambeg	Lambeg	800
1790	p. 636	John Hancock	Tulnacross [Tullynacross] Lambeg	Lambeg	2,000
1791	p. 184	William Ware	Skigoneil [Skegoneill]	Belfast	3,549
1792	p. 7	John Hancock	Lambeg	Lambeg	460
1793	p. 211	John Cambell	Edenderry	Belfast	6,080
1793	p. 48	Wm. Brown	Farm called the Throne, Ballygoland	Carnmoney	10,124
1795	p. 311	Val. Joyce	Farm called Rush-Park, Whitehouse	Carnmoney	680
1795	p. 914	Hu. Montgomery	Farm called Mount Vernon, Parkmount	Belfast	3,605
1795	p. 1015	Samuel Brown	Farm in Ballynafeigh	Knockbreda	1,835
1797	p. 784	Geo. Cubbison	Lands of Ballynafoy, Knockbreda	Knockbreda	6,901
1798	p. 792	Robert Bradshaw	Farm called Rosebank, White-Abbey	Carnmoney	3,878
1798	p. 691	Robert Getty	Farm in Skigonearl [Skegoneill]	Belfast	8,866
1799	p. 668	John Stewart	Lands of Lakefield, Parish of Belfast	Belfast	4,400
1799	p. 637	William Sinclaire	Lands of Ligoneil & Lower Ballysillan	Belfast	32,796
1799	p. 406	John Stewart	Lands of Lakefield	Belfast	4,400
1799	p. 318	Robert Getty	Farm at Sea-View	Belfast	12,515
1799	p. 204	William Legg	Demesne in Malone	Belfast	6,350
1799	p. 159	Hugh Crawford	Lands in the New Enclosure	Belfast	2,150
1800	p. 68	John Martin	Farm in Ballyhackamore	Belfast	7,407
1800	p. 873	Henry Haslett	Farm in White-Abbey	Carnmoney	6,200
1801	p. 88	Will. Irvin	Cromack	Belfast	1,100
1801	p. 130	William Sinclair	Lands of Skegoniel	Belfast	17,472
1801	p. 130	William Sinclair	Lands of Ligoneil & Lower Ballysillan	Belfast	4,700
1805	p. 223	Cunningham Gregg	Farm at Macedon	Carnmonry	5,500
1805	p. 224	George Bristow	Farm of Rose Lodge	Carrickfergus	8,324
1805	p. 1494	Isaac Thompson	Farm of Garden-Hill	Belfast	5,188
1809	p. 344	Samuel Alexander	Land at Edenderry, now called Brookfield	Belfast	5,570
1809	p. 424	William McCance	Lands at Dunmurry and Upper Falls	Belfast	8,750
1809	p. 452	Wm. Hunter	Lands of Dunmurry	Drumbeg	950
1810	p. 523	Arthur Reid	Lands of Old Park	Belfast	800
1810	p. 536	John McCance	Lands of Ballydownfine	Belfast	1,880
1810	p. 536	William McCance	Lands at Englishtown	Belfast	11,070
1810	p. 536	William McCance	Lands at Ballycullo	Belfast	3,034
1810	p. 508	William Hunter	Lands of Dunmurry	Drumbeg	1,700
1810	p. 200	George Cubbison	Lands of Ballymeghan	Holywood	5,808
1810	p. 228	William Simms	Lands called the Grove, Parish of Belfast	Belfast	3,870
1810	p. 640	William and Joseph Stevenson	Lands of Springfield, Edenderry	Belfast	2,167
1810	p. 640	William and Joseph Stevenson	Lands of Ballymagarry or Ballygarry	Belfast	9,012
1811	p. 967	Hugh McKibbin	Lands of Clownish, Parish of Belfast	Belfast	7,967
1812	p. 1052	John Kirkpatrick	Lands of Lisnabreen [Lisnabreeny]	Castlereagh	2,594
1813	p. 296	Alexander Mitchell	Lands of Brickfield	Newtownbreda	1,005
1813	p. 216	John McWatters	Farm in Aghalislone	Derryaghy	4,000
1813	p. 804	John McWatters	Farm in Augnalisloan [Aghalislone]	Derryaghy	4,200
1814	p. 446	Hugh Dunn	Lands in Strandtown	Holywood	1,328
1815	p. 956	William Thompson	Lands of Legoniel	Belfast	9,275
1815	p. 59	James Blair	Lands of Ballysillan	Belfast	10,687
1816	p. 218	John Cunningham	Farm in Whitehouse	Carnmoney	2,780
1818	p. 672	William Johnson	Lands of Fortfield	Belfast	2,200
1819	p. 91	Robert Greenlaw	Farm in Ballymaconaghy	Knockbreda	10,000
1819	p. 514	Hugh Crawford	Lands of Ballymoney, Ballydomfine [Ballydownfine] and Ballygammon	Belfast	2,250

Date and page in Dublin Gazette		Person registering trees	Location	Parish	Number of trees
1819	p. 574	John Garr	Lands of Lower Malone	Belfast	956
1819	p. 574	John Garr	Lands of Lower Malone	Belfast	1,350
1819	p. 591	John Thompson	Farm in Skigoniel [Skegoneill]	Belfast	2,900
1820	p. 101	James Blair	Lands of Wheatfield, Ballysillin	Belfast	4,100
1820	p. 475	Wm. John Hancock	Lands of the bleach green in Magherlea and Glenmore and Tullynacross	Derryaghy and Lambeg	914
1820	p. 531	Lawson Annesley	Farm in Ballysillin and Edenderry	Belfast	1,900
1820	p. 1024	Joseph Wright	Lands of Greencastle	Belfast	961
1821	p. 667	James Blair	Lands of Wheatfield, Balysillers [Ballysillan?]	Belfast	1667
1823	p. 200	William Boyd	Lands at Fort Breda, Breda	Knockbreda	2,756
1824	p. 273	Daniel Miskelly	Lands of Strandtown	Holywood	932
1824	p. 814	William Boyd	Lands of Fort Breda	Knockbreda	2,329
1824	p. 814	William Boyd	Lands of Galwally	Knockbreda	291
1826	p. 631	William Boyd	Lands of Breda	Knockbreda	4,498
1827	p. 521	John H. Houston	Ballyrushboy	Newtownbreda	2,912
1827	p. 391	James Blair	Lands of Wheatfield & Clearstream, Ballysillan	Belfast	1,100
1827	p. 815	Martha Berwick	Lands of Cregagh and Lisbabreeny	Knockbreda	3,800
1831	p. 42	Lawson Annesley	Lands of Derramore	Drumbo	2,700
1835	p. 267	John H. Houston	Lands of Knock	Newtownbreda	2,600
1838	p. 497	Andrew Jackson	Farms in Ballygraney	Holywood	1,300
1838	p. 345	Thomas McDonnell	Lands of Eglantine Hill	Belfast	823
1838	p. 328	Arbuthnot Emerson	Farm in Oldpark	Belfast	13,575
1840	p. 148	Horatio Maunsell	Lands in Ballylesson	Drumbo	1,012
1841	p. 138	John Byers Gunning and Robert Gunning	Lands in Ballygraney	Holywood	281
1842	p. 740	Arthur Crawford	Lands of Jordanstown	Carnmoney	3,852
1842	p. 954	John Feeney	Lands called Welsh's Glen	Carrickfergus	732
1843	p. 70	R. F. Gordon	Ballyrobert	Holywood	13,838
1843	p. 512	Robert Gunning	Lands of Ballygrainey	Holywood	749
1844	p. 176	R. F. Gordon	Ballyrobert	Holywood	17,072
1844	p. 492	Robert Gunning	Lands of Ballygrainey	Holywood	6,300
1844	p. 546	Thomas Sinclair	Lands of Ligoniel	Belfast	6,592
1845	p. 116	William Stewart	Lands of Jordanstown	Carnmoney	14,375
1845	p. 200	David Blizard	Lands at Ballyfinaghy	Drumbeg	1,500
1846	p. 327	R. F. Gordon	Ballyrobert	Holywood	7,800
1848	p. 395	Alexander Mackenzie Shaw	Lands of Wilmont and Forge Hill	Drumbeg and Belfast	14,603
1849	p. 284	Alexander Mackenzie Shaw	Lands of Wilmont and Forge Hill	Drumbeg and Belfast	7,714
1851	p. 394	Saml. Boyle	Lands at Ballymisert and Strandtown	Holywood	2,360
1851	p. 708	William Wetherall	Lands of Holywood	Holywood	17,670
1854	p. 159	William Simms	Lands of Rathfern	Carnmoney	12,739
1854	p. 109	John Coates	Lands of Ovoca Park, Ballyfinaghy	Belfast	8,237
1858	p. 1702	James Girdwood	Lands of Ballymisert	Holywood	3,345
1858	p. 1774	James Walker	The Knockagh, Troopers Land	Carrickfergus	12,000
1860	p. 1011	Robt. Bateson	Farm in Ballynavalley	Drumbo	3,877
1860	p. 1139	James Barnett J.P.	Farm in Malone	Belfast	2,220
1861	p. 748	W. J. C. Allen	Lands of Faunoran, west division of C'fergus	Carrickfergus	950
1866	p. 988	Robert Barbour	Lands of Glenmore	Lambeg	3,225
1867	p. 1234	James Greer	Lands of Gilnahirk	Knockbreda	1,675
1868	p. 104	Nathaniel Wood	Lands of Ballycloughan and Strandtown	Holywood	10,601
1869	p. 1256	R. G. Dunville	Lands of Knocknagoney	Holywood	18,410
1870	p. 1654	James Craig	Lands of Ballymisert	Holywood	3,163
1900	p. 1052	F. J. Robb	Lands in Lisnabreeny	Knockbreda	550

The above details of tree planting by tenants are a summary of records identified in a search of the Dublin Gazette. For further information about the number of each species of tree planted at each site and the name of the land owner, refer to the relevant year and page in the Dublin Gazette. Hand written versions of many of these records, together with more records never published in the Dublin Gazette, can be found in registers of trees for County Down and Antrim (Public Record Office Belfast reference DOW 7/3/2/1-3, ANT 7/6/1-2).

Appendix 4

Number of trees 3m or greater in girth at selected sites in Belfast

	Belvoir Park	Barnett Demesne	Cave Hill County Park	Purdysburn	Sir Thomas & Lady Dixon Park	Stranmillis
Native oak	130	54	-	29	33	8
Beech	47	50	15	26	37	30
Sycamore	15	24	25	10	29	11
Lime	14	21	3	3	13	1
Sweet chestnut	3	6	-	6	3	23
Horse chestnut	18	-	10	3	1	4
Ash	4	3	7		6	1
Turkey oak	4	2	-	1	1	2
Maple	-	-	2		2	-
Lucombe oak	3	-	-	-	-	-
Red oak	-	-	-	-	1	-
Holm oak	1	-	-	-	-	-
Non native conifers	26	4	30	3	20	1
Yew	5	-	-	-	-	-
TOTALS	270	164	92	81	146	81

Data from Simon, B (2005) A Treasured Landscape. The Heritage of Belvoir Park page 78 and from Simon, B (2008) A survey of Lowland Wood Pasture in Belfast Preliminary findings. This report, by the Forest of Belfast, is unpublished but the data has been placed on the Woodland Trust Ancient Tree Hunt database.

The survey of Belvoir Park covered the entire former walled demesne and Morelands Meadow. Barnett Demesne survey covered the park including Mary Peters Track and Queen's University land and housing area by Dub Lane. Cave Hill study covered all of the countrypark. Purdysburn survey covered the former demesne east of Hospital Road. Sir Thomas and Lady Dixon Park study covered the entire public park. Stranmillis survey covered the grounds of the college.

Picture credits

Front cover image:
Belfast Castle Estate by
Esler Crawford Photography.

p. 2 Illustration by Carol Baird for the
Forest of Belfast.

p. 6 Colin Glen by Esler Crawford Photography.

p. 10 Photograph by the author 2008.

p. 11 Photograph kindly provided by Roy
Anderson 2008.

p. 12 Illustration by Carol Baird for the Forest of
Belfast.

p. 14 Ulster by Frances Jobson. TCD MS
1209/17. Reproduced by kind permission of
the Board of Trinity College, Dublin.

p. 16 Map of Belfast Lough MPF 1/77.
Reproduced by kind permission of the
National Archives, Kew.

p. 17 Map of Belfast. Reproduced by permission
of the Linenhall Library.

p. 18 Raven maps. Reproduced by permission of
North Down Heritage Centre, Bangor,
County Down.

p. 20 Enclosing the deer park, Cave Hill. J W
Carey. Photograph reproduced courtesy the
Trustees of National Museums Northern
Ireland.

p. 21 Raven maps. Reproduced by permission of
North Down Heritage Centre, Bangor,
County Down.

p. 23 Illustration by Carol Baird for the Forest of
Belfast.

p. 24 Reproduced from Ulster Journal of
Archaeology, 1 (1853) pp. 58-62, 130-136.

p. 25 Photograph by the author 2008.

p. 26 Detail of Donegall estate map by Crow.
PRONI D/835/1/3/18. Reproduced by
permission of the Deputy Keeper of the
Records, Public Record Office of Northern
Ireland.

p. 29 Belfast from Cromac by J. Fisher. IB/1/772.
Photograph reproduced courtesy Trustees of
National Museums Northern Ireland.

p. 30 Belfast News-Letter 18-21 April 1786 p. 1,
11-15 August 1786 p. 1.

p. 31 Detail of Donegall estate map by Crow.
PRONI D/835/1/3/15. Reproduced by

permission of the Deputy Keeper of the
Records, Public Record Office of Northern
Ireland.

p. 32 Belfast from Friar's Bush by J. Nixon..
Photograph reproduced courtesy the
Trustees of National Museums Northern
Ireland.

p. 35 View of Belfast by J. Fisher. Image kindly
supplied by Christies, London.

p. 36 Belvoir House by J. Fisher. Image kindly
supplied by Christies, London.

p. 37 Aurora Photographic for the Forest of
Belfast 2008.

p. 38 Map of Malone Demesne PRONI
D/915/18/1. Reproduced by permission of
the Deputy Keeper of the Records, Public
Record Office of Northern Ireland.

p. 41 Reproduced from 'Taylor and Skinners Maps
of the Road of Ireland' (1777).

p. 42 Bullen's catalogue. PRONI T/3029/12.
Reproduced by permission of the Deputy
Keeper of the Records, Public Record Office
of Northern Ireland.

p. 44 Reproduced from Samuel Hayes 'Practical
Treatise on Trees' (1794).

p. 46 Belfast News-Letter 23 January1767 p. 2,
25 March 1768 p. 2, 21 August 1767 p. 2, 6
January 1815.

p. 48 Above: Belfast News-Letter 1-4 January
1782 p. 3, 24 March 1767 p. 2. Below:
Belfast News-Letter 26 August 1808 p. 1,
28 October 1828 p. 3.

p. 49 Photograph by the author 2009.

p. 50 Map of County Down by J. Williamson.
Reproduced by permission from a map held
by the Central Library, Belfast.

p. 53 Aurora Photographic for the Forest of
Belfast 2007.

p. 54 Detail of a map of Wilmont by Robert
Pattison (1842). Reproduced by kind
permission of the Linenhall Library.

p. 57 Photograph by the author 2008.

p. 59 Dufferin Estate map. PRONI D/2598/1.
Reproduced by permission of the Deputy
Keeper of the Records, Public Record Office
of Northern Ireland.

p. 62 Photograph kindly provided by Roy Anderson.

p. 63 Colin Glen by Andrew Nicholl. Reproduced by permission of Bridgeman art library (reference CH 342324).

p. 64 View of Glenavna. From 'Sights and Scenes in Ireland' Cassell and Company, London (1896)

p. 65 Belfast Castle. Lawrence collection new series 2520. Reproduced courtesy of the National Library of Ireland.

p. 66 Detail of a postcard.

p. 68 Northern Whig 4 August 1840 p. 3, 8 August 1840 p. 3, 2 September 1843 p. 3.

p. 70 Postcard.

p. 71 J. H. Connop's bird eye view of Belfast 1863. Reproduced by kind permission of the Linenhall Library.

p. 72 Ormeau Road by Hugh Thompson. Collection Ulster Museum, Belfast. Photograph reproduced courtesy the Trustees of National Museums Northern Ireland.

p. 74 Postcard.

p. 75 View of Belfast. From 'Sights and Scenes in Ireland' Cassell and Company, London (1896).

p. 76 Photograph kindly provided by Roy Anderson 2007.

p. 78 Postcard.

p. 80 Belvoir House. Reproduction of a slide by Douglas Deane. Monuments and Buildings Record, Built Heritage (NIEA), Hill Street, Belfast

p. 81 Air photograph of Stormont by Esler Crawford Photography.

p. 82 Postcard.

p. 83 Leaflet in Belfast Civic Society records. PRONI D/3760/1/7. Reproduced by permission of the Deputy Keeper of the Records, Public Record Office of Northern Ireland.

p. 85 Aurora Photographic for the Forest of Belfast 2008.

p. 86 Photograph reproduced by kind permission of the Belfast Telegraph.

p. 87 Illustration by Niall Timmins for the Forest of Belfast.

p. 88 Aurora Photographic for the Forest of Belfast, 2008.

p. 89 Photograph reproduced by kind permission of the Belfast Telegraph.

p. 91 Photograph kindly provided by Mark Hamilton 2009.

p. 92 Photograph kindly provided by the Woodland Trust.

p. 95 Photograph by the author 2008.

p. 96 Photograph by the author 2009.

p. 97 Image kindly provided by Mr Carson

p. 98 Aurora Photographic for the Forest of Belfast 2009.

p. 99 Photograph kindly provided by David Spence, NI Housing Executive.

p. 100 Photograph reproduced by kind permission of the Belfast Telegraph. Left to Right are Colin Brown (Roads Service), Maurice Parkinson (Head of Belfast Parks), a representative of Phoenix Gas (event sponsors), Ben Simon (Forest of Belfast) Frank Caddy (Belfast Chamber of Trade).

p. 102 Celebrating the planting of half a million trees. Lady Dufferin and Lindsay Brooke, wife of Peter Brooke the Secretary of State, plant an oak at Crawfordsburn Country Park. Reproduced by permission of Conservation Volunteers.

p. 103 Aurora Photographic for the Forest of Belfast, 2008.

p. 105 Illustration by Niall Timmins for the Forest of Belfast.

p. 106 Photograph by Markéta Janouchová. Reproduced by kind permission of Conservation Volunteers.

p. 107 Photograph by the author 2001.

p. 108 Photograph by the author 1990s.

p. 109 Illustrations by Niall Timmins for the Forest of Belfast.

p. 110 Photographs by the author 1990s.

p. 112 Photograph by Aurora Photographic for the Forest of Belfast 2008.

p. 121 Illustration by Niall Timmins for the Forest of Belfast.